UNDERSTANDING
THE HEART

Beyond the Façade

How to Perceive Through the Eyes of the Heart

CLINT HERREMA

Understanding the Heart—*Beyond the Façade: Seeing Through the Eyes of the Heart*

ISBN: 978-0-924748-48-6

UPC: 88571300018-5

Printed in the United States of America.

© 2010 by Clint Herrema

Rill and Associates
P.O. Box 119, Orrstown, PA 17244
303.503.7257

Cover artwork/concept: F. P. Bergamo
Exterior typesetting: Knail
Interior design and typeset: Katherine Lloyd

ENDORSEMENTS

"Most of us have at some point asked the question, 'How do I discern the difference between my own thoughts and God's voice?' In *Understanding the Heart* Clint Herrema thoroughly and biblically answers this question. This book is more than a good read; it is a ticket to understanding your heart. The result will be a more mature and genuine Christian walk."

—Dr. Duane VanderKlok
Lead Pastor, Resurrection Life Church

"Clint Herrema gives a detailed, written expression of clarity in his writing. He brings explanation to concepts that often are skewed and lost to the average believer. As I read this book, I gleaned greater revelation of things I thought I already knew. Grasping and comprehending simple truths of the Kingdom of God come alive with such personal connection to the Lord of our heart and life through Clint's book."

—Dennis & Denise Capra
Pastors and Co-Founders, Faith Ministries World Outreach Center

"'The Heart Doctor is in'…words you hope never to hear regarding the condition of your physical heart. When it comes to your personal relationship with a loving God, though—there are no better words to hear! God is using Clint Herrema (in *Understanding the Heart* or in this series) as 'the Heart Doctor'! Personally, my eyes have been opened to the reality of the heart and God's amazing grace. So, hop up on the table and let the Heart Doctor do a God surgery. You will be transformed!"

—Ted Mulder
Pastor, North Point Community Church

TABLE OF CONTENTS

INTRODUCTION

As you pour through this book, you will notice that it is written very differently than what you would expect. Since we are dealing with the heart, I have a great deal to address in the beginning steps, mainly due to the many faulty concepts that man and his religion have spread throughout history, which I cannot sidestep. In the beginning you will find many truths about the heart that will not be plainly spelled out. Bear with me! Much of what you will be gleaning can be enlightening in many areas, but my aim is to convey a much larger picture. In the end it will all come together and become part of a whole.

This book is second in a three-part volume. It is imperative that you grasp the precepts, or foundation, of the first half of this book prior to moving into the second part, let alone before moving on to the third and final volume of the series. If you do not take the time to slow down and digest this material, much of its message will be lost and there will be great potential for the heart of this subject to be skewed.

After laying down proper perspectives on what the heart is and the importance of its role in the life of man, we then can move, readily equipped, into the power of heart. The second portion of this book is where we will

7

dig into the power of the heart realm. It is where we will begin to enter into how we are to read our hearts, write on our hearts, establish, persuade, purify, examine, and guard our hearts. Ultimately, this teaching, combined with the knowledge from part one, is the area in which I pray you will find to be a door of freedom to living from the heart.

PART 1

The Precepts

THE CONCEPT OF HEART

*T*he heart is a subject with thousands of references in the Bible, yet with very little understanding as a whole within the body of Christ. It is one of the most pivotal elements to the makeup of man. Proverbs 4:23 in the New Living Translation tells us that the heart determines the course of our life. If we truly believe the Word of God, then it would make perfect sense for us to get an understanding of the heart in order to take control over the direction our lives are going. So, what is the heart? What are its functions? How is it different than our spirit? Why is it such an important component of our life? How do we examine, purify, establish, guard, listen to, and write on our heart? These questions may seem complex in the beginning, but I assure you that the process is quite simple.

When you *first* look into understanding the heart, it can seem very confusing and abstract—especially if it is compounded with our traditions and culture that have crept into much of our theology. The teaching on the heart is one of those areas that do not simply have a compounded structure to it. It is diverse in its presentation throughout the Bible, giving many glimpses into what the heart is, its function, and how it affects the whole of the spirit, soul, and body. As a result, I will address an assorted range of truths about the heart in Part 1 of this book in order to give you a good foundation for Part 2.

I LOOKED FOR ANSWERS IN THE WRONG PLACES

This is a spiritual field guide series, but when dealing with the heart there is a lot of groundwork to establish prior to getting into the how-to's. If we were to jump straight into the fundamentals right away, most of us would lose direction quickly and become overwhelmed with questions, which would detract from the lessons presented.

When I was a young boy growing up in the church listening to missionaries, evangelists, and even patriarchs within our own church, their amazing stories of faith would stir up in me a craving to have a dynamic walk with God much like Jesus had exemplified on earth. The problem was that I always felt like I was lacking something, as though I was insufficient for God to work through. I can remember thinking about what it must be like to have the miraculous Kingdom lifestyle as normal. What a wonderful life it would be—to speak the words like Jesus and others who portrayed that power through Him, to have all of creation yield to my authority in Him. What a wonderful walk that would be! But, the question remained, how do I "get there"?

As a child I always was watching and learning by what I observed more than by anything else. Children in general see and hear the messages we do not say solely by words. They watch our lifestyle, attitudes, and actions. They respond much by the way they feel. Babies are born into the world with only an instinctual understanding. They operate more out of an internal behavior; they are very attuned to subtle nuances and shifts within their heart and emotions. With time, as they grow and develop, so too does their logical and reasoning capabilities. It is these that the societies of man do a wonderful job at feeding and nurturing—until physical logic and reasoning is the dominating factor to all we focus and rely upon.

The societies of man do a wonderful job at feeding and nurturing our logical and reasoning capabilities.

My error as a child was in lacking the guidance and maturity to not focus on external measures alone. As I grew, my young mind only knew how to physically compare myself with the stories and examples I had witnessed.

In my comparison I looked on the external factors of what I wanted versus what (at that time) I perceived I did not have. It was a completely physical approach. I did not know how to perceive the heart. I as yet was unaware of the power that worked within people to make them the way they were and cause them to act the way they did.

I point this simple fact out to help you in the understanding of the heart. I questioned so much as a young boy because of the mixed messages I had then. I was told to believe and pursue the Lord wholeheartedly. I was told that God's will was for me to know Him just like Jesus knew Him. Yet, many of the ones who told me these things were not telling me from their own experience. It was obvious that they often recited what they had read from a scripture or two, but had no real substance of revelation from what they spoke. As my search to walk in the power of the Kingdom that Paul spoke of grew, so did my frustration and questions. "For the kingdom of God is not in word, but in power" (1 Corinthians 4:20 KJV). The questions I held were causing more frustration because I was searching externally for what could be answered only internally.

WE HAVE MORE THAN LOGIC

Society has trained us well in the area of logic. Our minds have wonderful analyzing capabilities. Very often we use our logical strengths to approach the Word of God, merely believing what our logic can comprehend. When in contrast the Word says that it is by faith that we understand (Hebrews 11:3). You see, first we believe, then we understand a matter. Not only that, but the Word also goes on to tell us that true understanding is not found within the brain but in the heart. The understanding we have in the brain is that of our logical reasoning abilities and is very limited to the physical world. The understanding of the heart is what opens our eyes to comprehend the unseen and eternal realities.

> *They have not known nor understood: for he hath shut their eyes, that they cannot see; and **their hearts, that they cannot understand.***
> Isaiah 44:18 KJV, emphasis added

*Who hath put wisdom in the inward parts? or who hath given **understanding to the heart?***

Job 38:36 KJV, emphasis added

*Trust in the LORD with **all thine heart; and lean not unto thine own understanding*** [don't lean on your carnal reasoning abilities].

Proverbs 3:5 KJV, emphasis added

Do not read into this more than what I am saying here. The logical mind is good and necessary for us to live in a physical world. But, man is not solely flesh. We are also spirit. So, we must walk within that duality of flesh and spirit. The logical mind alone is not enough for us to live complete in this life. It is not capable of bringing in the spiritual aspect of our existence. We must learn to harness and function within all parts of our composition. That is when we will begin to reach deeper into the realities of what Jesus continually taught and portrayed as our birthright in Him.

I am revealing the simple fact that we must become a people who once again are sensitive to the heart. There is what I call a "golden key" to understanding and comprehension; it is a vehicle through which we communicate with God. That "key" is the heart. In reference to the heart, Jesus laid out a parable for us in Mark chapter 4. It is what we could refer to as the heart parable. Not only that, but Jesus said if we could not grasp the principles of this parable on the heart, we would not be able to perceive all the other parables!

Then Jesus said to them, "If you can't understand the meaning of this parable, how will you understand all the other parables?"

Mark 4:13 NLT

GET READY FOR GREATER UNDERSTANDING!

We will walk through this heart parable in Chapter 5, "The Purpose of Parables," in much greater detail. By the time you are finished with this study on the heart, you will find it hard to read the Bible the same way. The understanding of the heart will begin to flow in your being, allowing you to see things as you never may have seen them before. The simplicity of the Scriptures will come alive; you will find it difficult to go back to your old way of reading those scriptures from a pure analytical approach. Prepare to have your personal theology rocked and have vigor return to your understanding!

Prepare to have your personal theology rocked and have vigor return to your understanding!

We, in our societies of mankind, stress the importance of reading, writing, and other physical academics to function in our world. A huge push is the need for literacy among our youth. There is nothing bad at all about this. In fact, being literate is a great asset and a command in the Bible. The only problem is that we have viewed literacy as only a physical issue. It is the literacy of the heart that this book is directed toward. The Bible tells us that we are to write on our hearts; examine and read what's in our hearts; and purify, establish, prepare, and guard our hearts. These are powerful commands, and Jesus is not going to do all of that for us. This is something we were given control over. The problem is that most of us are virtually clueless when it comes to these functions. We often are dumbfounded just trying to figure out and pinpoint what exactly our heart is.

These are the concepts and lessons we will be covering in this book. When you are finished with this book you will have an understanding of the heart at a level deeper than your logical mind can know. More than likely, you will have a very satisfying sensation of the new awakening within regarding the power of heart and its newfound concepts.

When the Bible refers to the "carnal mind," the "wisdom of the world," "fleshly wisdom," and so forth, it is referring to relating to the world only through physical measures. These are examples of being stuck in the vacuum of the physical logical mind, unable to comprehend the power and truth of the Spirit. Carnal Christians are those who only live according to their five physical senses, blinding themselves to the greater realities of the unseen and eternal.

As you begin to read through this book, please realize that I have many angles and views to address in the first part. There are many truths and concepts that will be discussed, which are all little pieces to a grand puzzle. In the end, however, they all will come together. To set out and discover the simplicity of the heart, you need to first gather up all of the seemingly loose ends that man's minds, along with religion, have created. As you set out upon this journey of discovery, know that there will be great reward in the end.

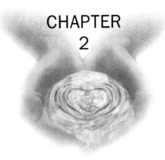

CHAPTER 2

THE PRECEPTS OF HEART

*W*hat is the heart? What is its function? Many would say that our heart and spirit are one and the same, that they are synonymous. When I was in Bible school I had professors say this, yet I also had others tell me that the heart was different than the spirit. I also understand that this is a newer concept to many. To understand why there are so many varied opinions on the heart we have to look at our history. There we can see what was lost and what is being restored to the church today.

There is one fact we need to keep in mind, though; and that is that we, the church, have gone through a period of a spiritual dark age. This is exposed in the basic truths that much of the church still argues over today. Even in Paul's day there were many who tried to change the message of the gospel of the grace of Christ by mixing in various laws as a requirement for acceptance with God. Even then the message of Jesus Christ and our identity in Him was challenged and polluted with carnal logic.

WHAT HAPPENED TO THE CHURCH?

According to Wikipedia, the concept of a "Dark Age" was first fostered by a writer named Petrarch in the 1330s. He used the concept of light and dark to describe the era in which there was light before and after a certain period. It was not an intended attack on Christianity, but rather an observation in which he believed the age of lack of knowledge was coming to an end. Later in the 16th and 17th centuries, Protestants saw the Middle Ages as a time of breaking away from Catholic corruption within the church. Lutheran scholars published a work called *Magdeburg Centuries* that reviewed church history century by century for the first 1300 years. They created a picture that painted the church as falling into great error after the fifth century.[1]

There always have been believers who walked in deep intimacy with the Lord. As I quickly review the church history, please understand that I am referring to the common beliefs of the religious leaders of those times.

The church has been going through a restoration process out from previous dark times. A great example today is the evidence when dealing with the Holy Spirit. In the early church we can find that the baptism of the Holy Spirit, accompanied with the gift of speaking in tongues, brought unity among the believers (Acts 11). Today Satan has twisted and confused many to a point where the baptism of the Holy Spirit accompanied with tongues is used to create division among the believers. Howbeit the Scriptures command us to forbid no one from speaking in tongues (1 Corinthians 14:39). I had family who suffered great persecution from their brothers and sisters in the Lord because they dared to believe in this baptism and the power of the resurrection flowing through the Holy Spirit. These family members were denied fellowship, business, and their children's friends.

Even with the native peoples of the Americas it is recorded that the European settlers believed such carnal doctrine that they thought God was killing the Indians with diseases so the English could move into their lands. John Archdale, governor of Carolina's province from 1694 to 1696, wrote: "And courteous Readers, I shall give you some farther Eminent Remark hereupon, and especially in the first Settlement of Carolina, where the Hand of God was eminently seen in thinning the Indians, to make room for the English.... it at other times pleased Almighty God to send unusual Sicknesses amongst

---

1 Wikipedia contributors, "Dark Ages," *Wikipedia, The Free Encyclopedia*, http://en.wikipedia.org/w/index.php?title=Dark_Ages&oldid=355895842 (accessed April 15, 2010).

them, as the Smallpox, etc., to lessen their Numbers...."[2] Later the Manifest Destiny came about in order to "civilize the savage Indian." Modern thought from the late 1800s through 1928 believed it necessary to "kill the Indian and save the man"; in other words, they were implying the removal of the "savage" from the Native American. This was accomplished through the use of much of the church. Missions were used as places where the government could send kidnapped Indian children in order to educate and civilize them before allowing them to return to their parents. To a large degree pastors and missionaries were greatly responsible as the ones who facilitated the destruction of the native peoples, a destruction that still has haunting effects today.[3]

I have many friends today who minister on Indian reservations. Their number one focus is to heal the people who were so greatly damaged by the carnal doctrine and actions done to Indian societies all in the name of Christ.

It is common to hear questions of what the early church used to look like. Division and segregation among the church body crept in according to whatever laws and rules were added to the grace of Jesus for righteousness. Fear and confusion abounded in doctrine and relationship with Father God. And if you really break down the differences of various Christian denominations, it all comes down to a different list or set of laws and rules. These are the devastating effects when we forget the words Jesus gave when He said the greatest of all commandments was love. The world will know we are His because we have love for one another.

The church has been going through a restoration process out from previous dark times.

Moving forward into the 1950s, it was a predominant thought that the soul and the spirit were not much different from one another. The common belief was that there was but a fine line between the two. Later, into the 1980s with the word of faith movement, people began to understand the

2 John Archdale, "A New Description of the Fertile and Pleasant Province of Carolina with a Brief Account of Its Discovery and Settling and the Government thereof to the Time, with Several Remarkable Passages of Divine Providence during my Time," 1707.
3 David Wallace Adams, *Education for Extinction - American Indians and the Boarding School Experience 1875–1928* (Lawrence, Kansas: University Press of Kansas, 1995).

concept of spirit and soul as having their own specific functions and different identity. Therefore they discovered that the two were not the same thing but very distinct. The understanding of our redeemed spirit man and joint union with Christ through our spirit was a great revelation of those days among believers, one that always will remain a foundation in understanding who we are in Christ. As for our day, we are standing on the shoulders of those who have gone before us, as we learn to bring the pieces back together as a whole. Today many are rediscovering the dynamics of the heart.

HEART VERSUS SPIRIT

The heart and spirit, until the recent turn of the century, were primarily discerned to be the same thing. So that would mean, according to this prior perspective, that you would read the words *spirit* and *heart* in the Bible and could interchange them to mean the same thing. In fact, this is how I was taught by my Sunday school teachers to read. The Bible is very specific about this, however; nowhere does it indicate that the spirit and heart are one and the same. "A new heart also will I give you, and a new spirit will I put within you" (Ezekiel 36:26a KJV).

The Hebrew word for "heart" in this verse is the word *leb*.[4] The Hebrew word for "spirit" is *ruach* or *ruwach*.[5] To make sure we are all on the same page I need to lay a little foundation. Look at the following passage.

> *Now may the God of peace Himself sanctify you completely; and may your whole spirit, soul, and body be preserved blameless at the coming of our Lord Jesus Christ.*
>
> 1 Thessalonians 5:23

Here it is very clear to see that we are a spirit, soul, and body. Paul is referring to our three-part being. I used to say, "I am a spirit, I have a soul, and I live in a body." The more I learn about my composition and the Word,

---

4 James Strong, *The Exhaustive Concordance of the Bible* (Nashville, Tennessee: Holman Bible Publishers, n.d.), #H3820.
5 Ibid., #H7307.

though, the more I have seen that I am a spirit, I am a soul, and I am a body. All three will be redeemed and glorified. Howbeit, I also have a heart. Yes, I am spirit, soul, and body, but I have a heart as well. Paul was not mistaken by leaving out the heart in this passage of scripture. It is up to you to purify and line up your heart to be congruent with His Word; it is not Jesus' responsibility. I can hear someone saying, "But doesn't the Word say I will be given a *new* heart?" Yes, if you believe on Jesus, then you have been given a new spirit and new heart; you have been made a new creature in Him. However, we often have let our guard down after the salvation experience and reprogrammed our hearts to line up with our old way of thinking. I will cover this more in Part 2 of this book. "Reprogramming" is what the Bible would refer to as writing on "the tablet of the heart." This is done through meditating on and then accepting a belief as truth, whether that belief is good or bad.

The heart is what we could call the control center of our being. Science has come to term, for the most part, what we know as the heart as the subconscious. There are many ways for me to describe this thing called the heart, especially due to its many functions. Another way we could interpret the heart is our core beliefs. The heart houses our absolute core beliefs—subconscious and conscious. You see, often we say one thing out of our mouths, but when the pressure is on something else comes out of our hearts. That indicates that although we desire to believe something, we still have heart work to do to transform our inner core beliefs.

The heart houses our absolute core beliefs –
subconscious and conscious.

Another way to describe the heart is as a valve, a conduit, or a doorway. It is the doorway to the spirit. Proverbs 4:23 in the New Living Translation says, "Guard your heart above all else, for it determines the course of your life." Your heart is the guiding system to what you will live in this life. I prefer the description of a valve. If you believe on Jesus as your savior, then you are righteous (2 Corinthians 5:21). Your spirit is sealed with the Holy Spirit (Ephesians 1:13). Your spirit is perfect and just (Hebrews 12:23). You are filled with the same spirit that raised Christ from the dead (Romans 8:11).

You are filled with eternal life! This eternal life is referred to as *ZOE* life. It is not a quantity of life, but a quality. You are filled with the very life that is in God (2 Corinthians 5:21; 1 John 4:13).

Your spirit is the part of you that has been redeemed (Romans 8:23; Ephesians 1:14; 2 Corinthians 5:17). You and I are waiting for the redemption of our soul and body. If you were to die and go to heaven tonight, you would not need a new spirit man if you believed on Jesus as your sacrifice. Your spirit is as holy, just, perfect, and righteous as it ever will get. So the question is, how do we live from the part of us that is redeemed? That, my friend, is through the doorway of the heart. It is the heart that sees and understands the unseen and eternal. Now, you will have to bear with me, as I will spend much of the rest of this book laying out this last statement.

Being a believer in Jesus and having a new spirit, the Bible says that you are sealed with the Holy Spirit. The Bible also says that you are the temple of the Lord. Think about this. Remember the ark of the covenant in the Old Testament? God inhabited the ark. Wherever the ark went, Israel saw great miracles and victory. The priests were to carry the ark into the river Jordan and immediately the waters parted. There are many stories about the ark of the covenant. Well, it is time to remove the blinders from our eyes. The ark of the covenant is actually an illustration of who you are today. New Covenant believers are in essence present-day arks of the covenant. When Jesus died, the veil to the holy of holies in the temple was torn in two. Until then, the ark of the covenant rested in the holy of holies in absolute seclusion from the world. But, God wanted to live in a temple not made by human hands. He wanted to live in you and me. Because God lives in you and me today, He is able to become mobile and invade planet Earth through us.

Think about the magnitude of this concept. This means that there is enough power in you to create an entire universe if need be. Not that you are going to do that, but the God who did create everything now abides in you. God, who is the Creator of everything around you and you personally, dwells in you, in your spirit. That quality of life is in you. But how do you access it? The golden key, as I will call it, is your heart. Your heart is like a valve to a giant reservoir. That reservoir is your spirit and the *ZOE* life within you. Your heart determines how much or how little of that life you will experience today.

This is why the Bible commands us to guard our hearts. If we allow people, lack, judgments, or bitterness to clog the life flow from our hearts, we will access very little of the Kingdom of God that is within us. Yep, I said within us. In Luke 17:21 Jesus said that if someone tells you that the Kingdom of God is over there, or over here, that we are not to go. He said that the Kingdom of God is within us. That is right; we have the Kingdom of God within us every minute of every day. It is an internal realm. The question is whether or not we will live within the riches of that Kingdom.

THE KINGDOM LIFE

Jesus said, "Enter by the narrow gate; for wide is the gate and broad is the way that leads to destruction, and there are many who go in by it. Because narrow is the gate and difficult is the way which leads to life, and there are few who find it" (Matthew 7:13-14). Jesus was not referring to heaven and hell in this teaching. Nowhere did He indicate that it was heaven and hell. So we cannot assume that. I truly and personally believe He was referring to the Kingdom of God. Consider this: Jesus says it is very easy to be accepted as a son of God by believing on Him and nothing more, but then here He says it is difficult? (See John 3:15-18.) Jesus was not confused about the Kingdom. It is easy to believe on Jesus and enter heaven after life on this planet. But, it is the entering the Kingdom lifestyle *today* that few will find. It is hard for us to lay aside our pride and opinions to embrace the Lord's view and opinions. Those who become like children, laying aside their egos, will be the ones who can enter the simplicity and power of the Kingdom life.

How many Christians do you know who understand and know how to enter the Kingdom of God that is within them? Most of us talk about the Kingdom and all the glory and stories about the Kingdom, but few really live there; much less know how to purposefully enter. First Corinthians 4:20 says, "For the kingdom of God is not in word, but in power" (KJV). When you begin to read the parables about the Kingdom of God in the Gospels with the understanding that Jesus was rarely referring to heaven when you die, but rather a realm that is within you, you will be amazed at the freshness and newfound depths of the Word.

IT IS YOUR CHOICE

The Kingdom of God is accessed only through the heart. The Kingdom is in the spirit. Like I said before, the heart is the gateway, or valve, to the spirit. You determine whether or not to go through that door with purity of heart and into the Kingdom. Truly, your heart is the real you. God looks at the heart of a man to know a man (1 Samuel 16:7). Your spirit may be redeemed and righteous in the eyes of God. That is wonderful to be accepted in the beloved as sons and daughters of the Most High. Howbeit, if God wants to intimately know you, your character, and your development of maturity, then He looks at the condition of your heart.

Let me finish with this. God ministers to your spirit; ministers and teachers minister to your soul (Hebrews 13:17); and you minister to your own heart. This statement may seem to be a stretch, but listen to what I am saying.

In Ephesians chapter 3 Paul prays that Christ would live in our hearts by faith. We have to choose to believe and persuade our hearts to allow Jesus and His grace to work in and abide in our hearts. Therefore, that is our choice, and ours alone. We have to decide what we will use to attend and minister within our own hearts. People can influence our heart through our feelings and emotions, but not without our consent.

Do you see what I am saying here? Only you decide what will or will not influence or dominate your heart and core beliefs. You have the power to harden your heart or soften it, whether to God and His Word or to your present circumstances and external inputs. No one controls what ministers to your heart but you. It is your responsibility to guard, establish, purify, and examine your own heart. You are in complete control as to what information you choose to listen to and embrace.

Only you decide what will or will not influence or dominate your heart and core beliefs.

Your physical senses constantly speak to your body. The Holy Spirit constantly ministers to your spirit and reminds you of your righteousness and position in Christ. Various teachers, friends, family, and outside influences speak to and influence your soul, but it is you who decides what will and will not enter into the core of your heart. You have the power of choice to experience either the life or death that encompasses all of life's decisions. In every situation and circumstance you live from your heart.

Whether conscious or not, we all live from within. We all are ultimately responsible for what we have hardened or softened our hearts to. We decide what we will use to meditate on and establish within our own hearts.

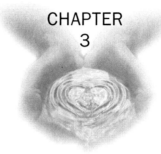

CHAPTER
3

DISCIPLESHIP

I must begin with the concept of discipleship. The word *disciple-ship* alone has been perverted in our modern-day interpretation. I am referring to the biblical model of discipleship that Jesus demonstrated with His disciples. Not, mind you, the discipleship that models after the world's philosophy that many of us have learned.

Before I move on into the comparison of the world's model versus Jesus' model of discipleship, please understand that I am blaming no one. Remember, we are still brushing off remnants of the dark ages. The Lord is always guiding His people out of religious strongholds and into the heart of the Father. This chapter is not meant to criticize or condemn anyone. It is simply here to open our eyes to the power of heart, and more importantly, to examine what the fruit of our contemporary Christian culture has produced.

This chapter rightly belongs to a time when the Lord was leading me into an improved model of discipleship, away from what I was practicing at the time. My wife Andrea and I had moved back to Michigan from St. Louis, Missouri. When we returned home to West Michigan after being away for nearly nine years, I had many people approach me in regards to discipleship. It was the strangest thing hearing their frustrations and near pleading for help in guidance from a spiritual mentor similar to an Elijah and Elisha type.

I was perplexed to hear so many old friends pull me aside and share how much they yearned to have what I had with Dave and Tom, two of my mentors. Some came with tears welling in their eyes, desiring a sincere and confident walk with the Lord. They just did not have anyone to walk with on that level and guide them further. They would share that when I told stories like hearing God call us to Ecuador, and that He would bring the contact to us on the plane, they were dying for that type of a relationship and confidence. This went on almost every day for nearly three weeks straight.

"IS MY FAITH FOR REAL?"

It was not until one person in particular said something that struck a nerve inside of me that I decided to give more attention to it. This guy took me out for dinner and we spent four hours talking. What he said was that he did not believe his faith would work in all environments. He shared an example of if he were dropped off in a jungle, desert, or some other desolate land without people, that he would panic at the mere thought. He said that his "religion" only seemed something that would work in the cities and societies of man, but not anywhere else. He said he learned how to interact with friends, family, and work environments. That his Christian studies showed him how to live in these practical scenarios, but he feared that if he were in a position of life and death, or something outside of his known environments, that his faith would not work. His concern was that he was living something that was based on circumstances more than a genuine lifestyle that truly knew and lived in the Kingdom of God. The bottom line was that he was living an external-based Christian philosophy.

It was through this friend that I realized how much we had in common. He was speaking something that I felt inside for nearly all of my life. I never wanted a walk of pretend Christianity, a walk that worked only long as everything was going right in my circumstances. I wanted that carefree lifestyle that knew I always would have safety and security in my savior, which was beyond logical comprehension. For the majority of my Christian life I have felt like I was very odd. I felt as though I desired things that I was not supposed to, like I was too radical in a sense for most. But, to me, if I could not know Him, then I would rather leave this earth and go home. Why live a lie?

I often felt that I had a thick head when it came to learning spiritual matters. For example, in Bible school people would always seem to hear God telling them this or that, but I was left with nothing. It was disappointing for me, and I figured I just was a bit on the slow side of hearing and learning. I used to hear people say amazing things God told them. It was even intimidating in a way. They apparently had a "direct line" with God, yet I struggled at having any confidence to believe when I thought I heard God's voice. It wasn't until years later that time proved many who claimed to hear God were speaking only from emotional hype and would eventually "flake out."

It took me years of practicing and learning to understand the simple truths that I will be laying out in this book. I spent months and years with mentors listening to their stories and putting into practice the lessons learned. I remember very well the week I had a major breakthrough in listening through the heart. It was so simple; but I had been over-complicating the language of heart and the means of listening. The breakthrough finally came when I quit complicating and over-analyzing that childlike belief.

> *I had been over-complicating the language of heart and the means of listening.*

Here now I was listening to others ask for someone to walk with on the spiritual path. I was hearing others ask for a walk with a friend and mentor for guidance to build up confidence and security in listening to the voice of the Holy Spirit. This was when the Lord began to unveil our modern methods of discipleship as those adopted by the world's system. He took me back in my memory to the times I felt the frustration of many I myself had discipled—where they seemed to walk strong with the Lord, only to fall away when difficulties arose in their lives. They would be doing so well, saying all the right scriptures, talking the talk, and yet lacking victory in their lives over adversity. When any adversity would come, they seemed to flounder in the chaos. Eventually they would walk away from the Lord, altogether blaming God for allowing these things to happen.

One thing I always have asked myself was that if my faith did not work anywhere and in any environment, then did I really have a faith to begin with? The next question I was led to ask myself was, "What changed since the early church?" Seriously, how could our methods of discipleship prove so weak and ineffective? Why were we losing so many people? What were we, as modern Christians, doing different than the early church?

THE FAITH OF THE EARLY CHURCH

Let's take a look at the contrast. Moving back in history to the beginning of what we know as the church age, Jesus had risen from the grave, conquered death, and redeemed us from the curse of the law. The church, or people of God, was growing at an exponential rate. Was it the anointed preacher who persuaded people of the day? Was it the perfection in articulation of speech and the latest technology? Of course not! There was clearly something else. But what?

Here was a time of great persecution. The world was rising up against the Christians and massacring them at an enormous rate. They made sport by feeding them to wild animals in the Circus Maximus. Families were butchered in front of one another while spectators jeered and laughed. In those days to be a Christian would have felt like the whole world was on fire. There was no real external "safety." Lands and homes were seized. Christians would move from one city to another in order to escape the persecution. A well-known fact of the "fish" or icthus, the symbol Christians often use for bumper stickers, originated from this first century church era. In the marketplaces it was far too dangerous to mention the name of Jesus, so Christians would draw the "fish" symbol in the dirt as a secret code to other Christians who might be nearby. This way they could identify who was safe to talk to and still have a sense of community.

I heard Andrew Wommack speak of his visit to the catacombs under Rome. One of the tombs had an inscription in the stone above, which read, "Here lays my wife and six month old daughter who gave their lives today in the Circus Maximus to the glory of Jesus Christ." He said that when he read it, he could feel the honor and passion of the husband. It was a feeling of how proud this man was of his wife and daughter, for the fact that they gave their lives for Jesus. How many of us contemporary Christians, I wonder, could say the same in that scenario?

Even further, it has not been uncommon to hear of a jailor or executioner receiving Christ after or prior to a sentenced execution. What is the quality of life these Christians possessed that caused others to desire what they had, even though they were considered to be worth disposing of in wretched manners? These executioners who had a change of heart recognized the fulfillment these Christians had in the midst of utter chaos. There was a life and sustenance they knew they had to find. Even though by confessing a faith on Jesus as Lord meant a death sentence, they would rather die and have life, than to go on living an empty, meaningless life among the "living dead." These Christians had the ability, like David, to offer up a sacrifice of praise to God in the midst of "hell."

So, what has changed from then to now? How were the early Christians able to locate and abide in the safe harbor, strength, and peace of the Kingdom within, while modern-day believers struggle to even find the secret place within? Why, when we experience an economic glitch in the country, do some of us lose houses in bankruptcy, lose businesses, or simply lose the surplus of finances and so turn away from God and fall apart like cheap material? Heaven forbid we actually may have hard times in our lives! History is full of examples where people faced hard times, lost earthly things, and even gave their lives. So why is it now that dollars are so powerful that we would rather serve our wallets than God? Have we truly lost the ability to abide in the secret place with the Almighty, that place of heart? Have we lost our way to peace and everlasting joy? I thought our God was not the source of problems, but the answer to them? Why are the believers of today, as a whole, so drastically different from the early church?

Why are the believers of today, as a whole, so drastically different from the early church?

I am trying to hammer the point that if things go wrong in your life, that does not indicate that God is in some way angry with you or that you are doing something wrong. If that were the basis for knowing if you are doing things right or wrong, then Paul must have lived most of his life out

ill of God, along with many of the other early apostles, not to men-
sus Himself. God promised to never be angry with you again! God is
wrathful; He is Love. He had wrath for disobedience, but that wrath was
en away on the body of Jesus for those who believe. In the same light, if
everything is going right in your life, it does not necessarily signify that you
must be doing something right. Even more so, it doesn't mean God must be
happy with you. If Christians believe this way, then they have one foot in the
Old Covenant and one in the New Covenant. That belief system will make
you one flakey Christian, with a very schizophrenic god.

Again, I must emphasize: I believe God for the best. I do not expect the
worst. However, if bad things happen upon me, I am confident in my Lord
to lead me out of them. I have witnessed His faithfulness and quality of life
where most would perish. Paul even warned us that if we desire to live godly
in Christ, then we would suffer persecution. Peter said not to think it strange
when hard times or persecution arises. They come to steal the Word and life
that God has given and placed within us. I always believe God for the best
in any situation or environment. That is my hope. We are prisoners of hope,
as Zechariah puts it. So I am not a gloom and doom preacher, but rather a
minister of life! I am a minister of the gospel of hope and good news! When
bad things happen, you and I have a savior and a hope in Him that the world
could never know.

STUDENT OR DISCIPLE?

*These likewise are the ones sown on stony ground who, when they hear
the word, immediately receive it with gladness; and they have no root in
themselves, and so endure only for a time. Afterward, when tribulation or
persecution arises for the word's sake, immediately they stumble.*

Mark 4:16-17

Now, these verses were taken out of the parable of the sower and the
seed. There were four soil conditions Jesus used in this parable, one of which
was stony ground. Jesus referred to soil as the heart. He also referred to the
seed as the Word of God. The intent of the "seed" was to land on the soil so

it could grow. In other words, the intent of God's Word is to be planted deep and firm within your heart, for what you allow in your heart is what will grow and mature.

Jesus said some great statements here that describe our modern sense of discipleship. He said that the seed that landed on stony ground referred to people who heard the Word of God with great joy. But, there was one problem. When the trials, persecution, and difficulties of life came, these people would "flake out" and fall away.

What you allow in your heart is what will grow and mature.

First, notice that tribulations and persecutions come for one reason only. That reason is to steal the Word from your heart so that it does not germinate, grow, and bear fruit. Did you notice, though, that the Word in this example of the stony heart never made a solid root in the heart? This reflects the disciples and hearers of the Word who mentally catch the Word in their own carnal logic, but they never allow their heart to embrace it as a core belief. That is why they receive it with joy! It makes sense, and it is exciting to hear the promises of God and His favor and love towards us. They embrace the Word as long as it does not challenge their personal opinions and logical reasoning. But, when trials come, these people say to themselves that they did not sign up for difficulties, so they abandon the Word looking for the easy way out. Thus they go back to the philosophy of the world they once knew so well.

A "hard" heart simply means it is hard toward one thing yet soft toward another. If a heart is stony or hard toward the Word of God, that would indicate that although the hearers may like the Word, they do not esteem it as supreme in their life.

Let me explain it this way. In the physical world's philosophy of discipleship, you pay a tuition; the "masters" of that profession give you all the answers; you take exams; and with a little time, presto! You now have achieved any degree you wish. What did it prove? It proved the fact that you have a good memory. That is why so many people with PhDs have little common sense. In some cases there was slight demand on passion. There was very little to do with internalizing the lessons and concepts of a truth in the student's life prior to building upon the next truth.

Does this sound familiar to you yet? In spiritual training people have taken much of the same approach. You pay tuition; I give you all the important scriptures to memorize. Then you learn arguments and methods to win someone to the Lord. Once you have proven to say all the right answers, look good, and polish up externally, you are awarded with the recognition of a well-trained disciple and now reproduce the cycle with someone else. There's just one problem: In so doing, you and I have neglected the heart.

The disciple from the parable of the sower and the seed in Mark chapter 4, regarding the stony heart, is the example I have just given. You see, I had done this with so many of my own disciples. I focused on giving them all the right scriptures. I spoon-fed them all the answers. I helped them to learn arguments that would win anyone to the Lord, not requiring them to put in the much-needed practice and passion to learn on their own and overcome obstacles. I even helped teach them how to flow in the supernatural gifts of the Holy Spirit by the grace through Jesus. I basically created little perfect models out of the brain. I, in essence, was making disciples of the logical mind.

It was not my intention to neglect the heart. I just was doing what I was taught to do. This model worked for a few, but not the majority. Not everyone has the same passion I do; nor does everyone learn the same and have the same background. This is why it is of the utmost importance to have someone disciple and train others from the heart and not the intellect. We have made teaching and mentoring all about the transference of information, and rarely about experience and knowledge through the heart.

I heard Dr. Jim Richards put it in perfect words. He said that we as a church whole have created students and not disciples. Students want information; disciples pursue transformation. A student says, "I want to know what my teacher knows." A disciple says, "I want to live like my teacher lives." This is why in Bible school you can see so many students learning and building their logical intellect, yet still living in utter chaos in their personal lives. There is no freedom in mere information. It is how one applies and uses the truth that sets one free into effortless transformation. Knowledge is not wisdom! In our Christian culture it is common to know more about God than it is to know God Himself.

Then Jesus said to those Jews who believed Him, "If you abide in My word, you are My disciples indeed. And you shall know the truth, and the truth shall make you free."

John 8:31-32

Jesus is saying here that the earmark of disciples is the fact that they are experiencing freedom. He did not say they will be perfect in their flesh. He said they will abide in His Word and the Word, or truth, that they know will make them free. It is not just the fact you can reason the Word that makes you free. You have to know that truth intimately. Feel that truth; let it become part of who you are. Abide or dwell within that Word; see it and how it impacts your life. Embrace that Word and allow it to become part of who you are. It should become part of the fabric of who you are. That Word should influence you from the inside out. Then, and then alone, is when that Word will come alive and begin to set you free.

The litmus test for me to see if someone is walking as a disciple or a student is to listen to his or her talk. I watch the person's life. It doesn't take long for me to see and hear if he or she is someone who just acquires knowledge or someone who is walking out the process of change and transformation by the truth he or she has been given.

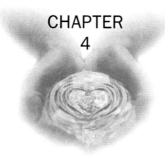

CHAPTER
4

TO SEE, OR TO
SEE AND ENTER?

Jesus replied, "I tell you the truth, unless you are born again, you cannot see the Kingdom of God." "What do you mean?" exclaimed Nicodemus. "How can an old man go back into his mother's womb and be born again?" Jesus replied, "I assure you, no one can enter the Kingdom of God without being born of water and the Spirit."

John 3:3-5 NLT

This passage of scripture clearly lays out the fact that the born-again experience is not one and the same as entering, or walking within, the realm of the Kingdom of God. In the physical world, when a person is born, he or she does not automatically grow and mature into an adult. There is a process involved. A baby is nurtured, cared for, and trained to live within the environment around him or her. So, too, is the world of spirit. It is after we are born into the Kingdom of God that I want to focus on. Just because someone has been born again by believing on Jesus, does not mean that that person automatically will walk in maturity and function to his or her full potential within the realities of the Kingdom. Many people have been born into the Kingdom of God. But, many will never know the life and rapture of that Kingdom. They will have a righteous spirit and unlimited access to the Spirit, yet no understanding of the power and quality of life within that Kingdom environment.

Often in our tradition of reading the Word of God, separated from the concept of the composition of man, we wrap everything up into one category. We read the Scriptures as if each verse stands alone apart from the rest of the Bible. It is paramount that we read the Bible as a whole and learn to divide the Word of truth into what it is saying in detail. For example, a scripture may refer to your soul and not your spirit man. But if you interpreted that verse by thinking it meant spirit, soul, and body all wrapped up in one, you would experience great confusion.

THREE GUIDING LIGHTS

As we enter this realm of dividing heart and spirit I feel compelled to give what I call the *three guiding lights*. As we divide the Scriptures, it is absolutely paramount that we interpret a scripture by some sort of guidance system so we don't get off track. These guiding lights, as I call them, are from the idea of a guidance system used in ancient times for ships entering a harbor. When a ship came into a harbor during the night, there were three torches lit that the captain used as his guiding system. If the torches lined up and looked like one torch, then he knew he was going the right course. However, if the captain could see all three or even two, then he knew he had to turn the vessel in order to see them all lined up as if one.

> *It is absolutely paramount that we interpret a scripture by some sort of guidance system so we don't get off track.*

These guiding lights, or torches, for reading the Word of God are very simple. First is the life and ministry of Jesus. What we see in the Scriptures that pertain to us as New Covenant believers must line up with the life and ministry of Jesus and what He exemplified on earth. Second is the finished work Jesus accomplished on the cross. Jesus accomplished a great work through His death, burial, and resurrection. If what we are reading in a scripture contradicts the finished work of Jesus, then we are misinterpreting the Word or looking at an old, obsolete covenant. Thirdly, the last torch is the position of the New Covenant believer. Again, if we read something in the Word that is contrary to our current position in Jesus Christ, then we must reevaluate what we are reading. These three always must line up in what we are studying or reading. If one is off, then we must allow ourselves the grace to know we do not properly understand that scripture. For me there was just such a scripture, one that baffled me for more than ten years, which I will share in Chapter 5.

RIGHTLY DIVIDING TRUTH

*Be diligent to present yourself approved to God, a worker who does not need to be ashamed, **rightly dividing the word of truth.***

2 Timothy 2:15, emphasis added

Before I move on, allow me to demonstrate what I was saying in the previous paragraph. I referred to rightly dividing the Word of truth, then followed up with this scripture from 2 Timothy 2:15. What I referred to was correct, but often we read so quickly that we don't take the time to digest what the true message is within our heart's understanding. Logically, we can speed read and hear what God was saying. But on the surface it would sound something like, *"Be diligent to show God how committed you are, by being a hard worker and not lazy. That you will be a know-it-all when it comes to the Bible. It is then that God will be happy with you."*

Obviously, I exaggerated this first interpretation to make a point. For many whom I have spoken with about this scripture, though, they have interpreted this verse not much different. That is the way it would read if we solely used our intellect to do all the thinking for us without incorporating some standard through which to read scripture. Now when I read that and hear an interpretation conveyed to me like what I just quoted, within my heart I get a wrong feeling. Even though I may not be able to articulate what that feeling is, I know it is an incorrect interpretation; there is something missing. It is then that I *"rightly divide"* the Word and look at the whole. I must make sure all three guiding lights line up.

There is nothing more I have to do in order to earn brownie points with God. So, I know that the verse in 2 Timothy is not saying this is what I must do to make God happy with me or else…. If, however, I were to look at this scripture and how it works in light of the work Jesus finished on the cross, my stance as a believer within this New Covenant, and with what Jesus modeled for me when He was on earth, then this verse would sound something like this: *"It is your job to be diligent and prove to yourself through the Word that you are already approved and loved by God! There is no need for shame, guilt, or condemnation, but you must put forth effort to see that perspective. This is how to divide the Word of truth."*

I know this is radical for some, but it lines up with our freedom through the life of the Spirit of Christ. We are free from the performance trap in which the letter of the law could not work the needed righteousness in our lives for freedom's sake. I am not saying that we go and live sinful lives because of our freedom in Christ. That would be just plain stupid.

Going back to John 3:3 where I started, I want to address a couple of things. First, the Kingdom of God is not necessarily the born-again experience. In fact, Jesus said that you cannot even see, or perceive, the Kingdom if you have not been born again first. Then He goes on to say that you cannot even enter the Kingdom of God until you have been born again. That would mean that you could see the Kingdom after you are born again, but not necessarily mean you would automatically enter into the Kingdom of God.

I can see some of you already getting a little lightheaded from this last statement, but let me go on. Just because you have been born again—which means you have a brand-new spirit, are the righteousness of Christ, and are going to heaven when you leave planet Earth—does not mean you are automatically functioning in the realm of the Kingdom of God. You see, when the Bible talks about the Kingdom of God or the Kingdom of heaven, it is referring to a realm as well as a provision of that realm.

*That **whoever believes in Him should not perish but have eternal life.***
For God so loved the world that He gave His only begotten Son, that
whoever believes in Him should not perish but have everlasting life.

John 3:15-16, emphasis added

Here is an example of the Kingdom and righteousness in two different passages. John 3:15-16 speaks about how simple it is to receive eternal life, or *zoe* quality of life. How easy it is to not perish but go to heaven as righteous when you die by simply believing on Jesus. Jesus was referring to the born-again experience and being filled with the God quality of life, having the Kingdom of God in you. If you read the verses before and after John 3:15-16, they continue to hammer in the simplicity of no more condemnation for those who receive Jesus as their savior and as the sacrifice by which they come to God with. He, Jesus, is the perfect sacrifice; there is no more wrath towards you because Jesus' payment was doubly sufficient for your sins, making you righteous in the eyes of God.

Enter by the narrow gate; for wide is the gate and broad is the way that
leads to destruction, and there are many who go in by it. Because narrow
is the gate and difficult is the way which leads to life, and there are few
who find it.

Matthew 7:13-14

But, then how do we view this passage about the narrow and difficult gate leading to the life, which states how narrow and difficult it is to enter into this *zoe* quality of life? It goes on to say how wide the gate to death is and that that is where the great majority of people will go; very few will be able to find the narrow, difficult gate to life. Most of us have interpreted this verse as implying only heaven and hell, as being born again or not. That is a partial translation. Jesus was not confused when He said that it was as simple as believing on Him to be saved, but then said it is much more complex and complicated than believing on Him. It may sound that way when we view this scripture alone. (I cover more of this in a later chapter.) Deuteronomy 30:19 acknowledges the choice we have every day in every moment of every hour whether to choose life or death. In any circumstance or environment, there is life and death. The negative may seem to outweigh the positive; nonetheless, life still abounds.

It is often difficult for us to let go of our physical personal perspective of the death all around us, but we are commanded to submit ourselves to God without bias to any circumstance. If we submit to God, then we will always be submitting to life. James 4:7 says we are to submit ourselves to God and resist the devil, and the devil will flee. Often it is easier to submit to the death and chaos and resist life and peace. Death and chaos do not require personal attention. If things are let go to tend to themselves, they will go into disorder. To resist the devil, we also resist the thievery, murder, and destruction that come with him. It is easier to take a victim mentality, roll over with the punches, and just accept them in our lives. Yet, to submit ourselves to the abundant life we have through God, we often have to make a conscious decision to stand patiently believing the best in any situation. Often it takes effort to see the life and potential in a negative scenario. Only God can turn things good from what the enemy meant for our destruction. God is hoping you will choose life each and every day.

Remember, God never uses evil or affliction to draw us to Him. Romans 2:4 says it is the goodness of God that leads men to repentance. Again, 2 Timothy 3:16 says God uses His Word—not problems—to correct or reprove us. Afflictions are what Satan uses to try and steal the Word from us (Mark 4:16-17).

All of salvation operates by the same principles (Colossians 2:6). We enter the life and experience of the Kingdom of God in the same manner as when we first were born again: through believing. The believing accessed the grace that already was made available to us. Howbeit, there are many Christians today who are able to believe on Jesus for their eternal salvation, but who find it difficult to believe anymore to live and encounter everyday salvation for the here and now (2 Corinthians 6:2). Matthew 7:13 not only refers to believing on Jesus for heaven, but also refers to entering the salvation that belongs to us for today in the form of peace, joy, safety, protection, prosperity, and so on for the body and soul. All of salvation is based upon believing on Jesus. What makes it difficult to enter that simplicity of believing is our desire to earn salvation based upon our own merit. We are just like the Isra-elites, who in Deuteronomy 6:25 declared that their performance and good works would earn their righteousness. So instead of the *gift* of righteousness, they wanted God to *owe* them righteousness.

Yes, what I am saying is that many people who are born again will never mature into knowing the depths of Kingdom of God that is within them. If you look around, you will be able to see the evidence of that everywhere. Very few Christians actually live and operate in the Kingdom, reaping the rewards Jesus provided for us today. Most Christians who proclaim Jesus as their sav-ior have little difference in their lives from those who don't pronounce Jesus as their savior. Have you ever wondered why?

> *But seek first the kingdom of God and His righteousness, and all these things shall be added to you.*
>
> Matthew 6:33

Notice what Jesus said here. You are to seek the Kingdom of God *and* His righteousness. These are two different things. You are righteous by believing on Jesus alone. It is entering the Kingdom of God that many fail to do. In Christ you are righteous; you have unlimited access to the Kingdom of God. Before you were born again, you had your own righteousness, which could never open the door for you into God's Kingdom. It is Jesus' righteousness that gives you the access to the inheritance of the saints, which furthermore is based upon Jesus' rewards for His perfect obedience. The saints refer to you and me!

It is crucial that I begin to dissect the Kingdom of God and the born-again experience to help you start this process and journey into understanding the heart. I have run into countless Christians who are tired, burned out, and frustrated with what they know as the Christian walk. Most struggle with the confusion of seeing the Kingdom, or seeing the promises of God, but lacking the application and experience. They can't seem to enter into the Kingdom lifestyle, as is their inheritance. It is a vicious internal battle between the logical mind and the pure mind of the spirit. It is now that you and I are ready to dive into depths of truth not only to see, but also to enter the Kingdom of God.

WHAT ARE WE ENTERING?

And He said, "The kingdom of God is as if a man should scatter seed on the ground, and should sleep by night and rise by day, and the seed should sprout and grow, he himself does not know how. For the earth yields crops by itself: first the blade, then the head, after that the full grain in the head. But when the grain ripens, immediately he puts in the sickle, because the harvest has come."

Mark 4:26-29

The Kingdom of God is not something that we just jump right into and instantly have *all* of the fruit working in our lives! Jesus said the Kingdom of God is like planting a seed. That seed then takes the time to germinate, sprout, grow, and mature. Then the fruit ripens, and it is at that time we reap. It is a process! Now, some processes take only a few moments. Others may take days. But much of that depends upon the condition of the heart one is working with, much like Jesus described in Mark 4. The process has everything to do with our hearing, believing, perceiving, and ultimately our understanding. As Andrew Wommack likes to say, "Have a need? Sow a seed."

Before I can go into the "how to enter," I must deal more with what it is we are entering into. The Kingdom of God is a realm as well as a provision of that realm, as I have mentioned before. You could think of it like Einstein's theory of parallel realities. It is another reality. But what exactly is that reality? Here's how Paul summed it up: "For the kingdom of God is not eating and drinking, but righteousness and peace and joy in the Holy Spirit" (Romans 14:17).

The Kingdom of God is a realm as well as a provision of that realm.

If you are anything like me, you would have heard that the Kingdom of God is righteousness, peace, and joy in the Holy Spirit and thought to yourself, *What does that mean?* Paul's letter to the Romans was written to the Christian Romans of his day; it was not directed to you and me in our modern English. Paul wrote in a language those people would understand.

The truth has not changed; we just need to take a moment to digest what he was saying.

To say that the Kingdom of God is righteousness, peace, and joy in the Holy Spirit is quite a mouthful. Paul is not referring to some boring religious talk that sounds good and holy. He is making a powerful statement that has many layers to reveal. First, let's look at righteousness.

Righteousness in the Holy Spirit means you have been sanctified and sealed by the Holy Spirit. You are justified and in perfect standing with God. There is no more separation standing between you and God. You are literally as righteous as Jesus (2 Corinthians 5:17). You are now walking on planet Earth with the same spirit inside of you that raised Christ from the dead. You have the Comforter with you at all times, whether you feel like it or not. That righteousness gives you complete right and authority to function just like Jesus—because it is Jesus' righteousness and authority, and He gave it all to you! You are in Him and He is in you. Jesus did the work and you receive the rewards from His work.

> *He who receives a prophet in the name of a prophet shall receive a prophet's reward. And he who receives a righteous man in the name of a righteous man shall receive a righteous man's reward.*
>
> Matthew 10:41

This is exactly what happened when you received Jesus! You received His rewards! All the rewards and inheritance Jesus has are now yours. As He is, so are you in this world (1 John 4:17)! This righteousness is no small thing. When you function out of this reality and state of being, you are beginning to walk in a completely different dimension than the rest of the world. They cannot even understand what kind of power you are dealing with here.

Let's go further and look at peace. Jesus said that you have His peace and that He will never remove His peace from your life. "Peace I leave with you, My peace I give to you; not as the world gives do I give to you. Let not your heart be troubled, neither let it be afraid" (John 14:27). This peace is radical! This is not a peace that means being free from external conflict. It is a peace that goes beyond anything the physical world could understand.

It literally means nothing missing and nothing lacking. The Bible also says that you shall not lack because God never leads you into lack, nor is there any lack in Him. Peace here is referring to spirit, soul, and body. It is an absolute oneness…no barriers between you and God…nothing stands in the way any longer, nor can anything ever come between you and Him.

This peace will manifest greatly within your heart and soul. Conflicts, adverse circumstances, persecutions, and the like may arise that may be out of your control, but you will always have control over continuing to experience the peace and joy or experiencing devastation and fear. Because this peace is not based upon an award system, you can access it whenever you need. You can decide to live always in this peace that produces a quality of life that money, sex, drugs, or any other worldly good can never come close to providing.

The peace Jesus gives is a peace that, like righteousness, frees us from any fear and shame. It gives us boldness to always approach God and know that we are accepted no matter what mistakes we have made in our lives. God is a spirit and He looks at us after the spirit. He is not focusing on our physical person. God looks at us based upon the sacrifice.

In the Old Testament, before Jesus came and redeemed man from the curse of sin and death, God required that blood be shed for the sin of man. At least once a year people would go to see the priest. At that time he would offer a sacrifice of a lamb for the sins of the family. The blood of that lamb atoned only those sins for the past year. It only temporarily made atonement for the sins of the family. When the priest was given the sacrifice of the lamb, the priest never once questioned the family as to what they did wrong. He never asked how bad their sins were. Never did the priest *examine* the people. Rather, the priest's job was to *examine* the sacrifice. He inspected the lamb to make sure it was a perfect specimen. He checked to make sure it was healthy and free of broken bones. In essence, he checked to make sure it was a worthy sacrifice.

That is the Old Testament example of how God looks at us today when we come through Jesus! The lamb represents Jesus. God does not examine us, but rather Jesus. He sees Jesus as a perfect sacrifice by which to enter into His Kingdom. Thus, we have an amazing peace that is much more than a peace known to the world. It is a supernatural peace of confidence and fulfillment that allows us unlimited access to the throne of God and His Kingdom.

Last, but not least, is joy. Joy is better said as an "everlasting joy." It is not a joy or happiness based upon external circumstances working to our benefit. Nor is this joy necessarily a happy, bubbly, smiley, obnoxious type of joy manufactured by human emotions. It is a joy of overwhelming satisfaction and deep internal fulfillment. Regardless of any environment, this joy is deep within the heart of every believer. Many live their entire lives never knowing this joy. It is like a fountain that can be experienced any time of day or night. This joy can be found only in the Spirit of God. It is far beyond human comprehension. Often, we can't even put words to articulate the satisfaction and joy within, but we know that something has changed in our spirit.

The Word says that the joy of the Lord is your strength. Joy gives you the strength to walk through any adversity. It is only when you are depressed and discouraged through deceit that the enemy can attempt to devour you. Joy puts a spring in every step; it is birthed from confidence that God is on your side and fighting for you. It is a fruit of knowing your identity as a child of the living God. When you truly believe in your core that you are who God says you are, no one can remove your joy or manipulate you into performance to prove your value or worth.

Why is the Kingdom of God summed up as righteousness, peace, and joy through the Holy Spirit? The answer is because all of the realm of the supernatural is available to us through these three. Love is made evident because of what our righteousness entails. For God so *loved* the world He made righteousness a gift, through the best He had: Jesus (John 3:16; Romans 8:32). Joy is manifest because of faith. An earmark of faith is that joy is always present. For example, I shared a story of a near-death experience from a brown recluse spider bite in my first book, *How to Release the Power of Faith*. The night I got a revelation and saw the end—healing—from the beginning of my prayer, joy was bubbling within my spirit even though I only had the answer through faith. It was not an obnoxious happy joy, but a deep state of joy in my core that emerged through the absolute belief when I used the name of Jesus. Finally, peace is a must to enter any relationship, much less the Father's. If we have animosity or strife between us and someone else, there can be no depth to that relationship. All the miracles Jesus did were through this Kingdom veracity. The relationship He had with Father God was again through this Kingdom reality.

Imagine a realm where there was an atmosphere or an ambiance of this righteousness that wrapped all around you everywhere you went. Experience a realm where the presence of peace was so thick that it permeated every fiber of your body through your imagination. Sense that peace beyond any description of words, where you could not even conceive a feeling or idea of what it is to lack. Feel that place, touch it; now feel the joy that comes with everything described. Feel the confidence and assurance you have from there. Now, be aware of and experience the dignity and honor you have been given; feel the purpose in your life. It is from this realm of existence that you are called to live, to know, and walk with God your Father. Only from that place can you ever hope to touch and heal a dying world. You have to see the end from the beginning. Most people are not experiencing this life within, so there is not much external difference between them and the world.

Righteousness, peace, and joy at the depth of what Paul was referring to are found only in the Spirit of God. People have asked me in times past about listening to the Lord in prayer. Some have made accusations that I must be careful because a deceiving spirit may try and act like God's voice. As always, I point to righteousness, peace, and joy. When God speaks to me there is no confusion, fear, anxiety, unsettledness, or disunity with His Word. By knowing and abiding in a state of righteousness, peace, and joy, no one can deceive you. Like Jesus said in John 10, "My sheep know My voice." As we establish ourselves in the authenticity of the Kingdom of God, we grow in our innate ability to spot a fake a mile away. When God speaks it is natural, fluid, peaceful, calming, and assuring, almost like a velvety-like feeling. Why? Because we were made and designed to hear His voice. It is supposed to be natural and right to know and hear our Father's comforting voice. These are the attributes of God, and He will strengthen and confirm them. They cannot be discovered by intellectual achievement. Knowledge does open our eyes to what is there; howbeit, knowledge cannot bring us into those realms. It is like a seesaw effect. As we grow in knowledge, we also must grow with experience and application of that knowledge. If we only grow in knowledge, we will deceive ourselves into thinking we have ascended to all that is possible, but we will lack the living aspect.

"LORD, LORD..."

One example I would like to use in regards to understanding the heart for reading parables is a scripture that scared me for years. I always have yearned to learn and teach spiritual laws and principles that work. There is logic in all that God does; that logic is called the *Logos* of God. You know it as the *Word* of God. A plus B must equal C! There is an equation, but there is no one method. Truth is always truth, but that truth always is applied uniquely in each given circumstance. This is where wisdom comes into play. That may make your head go tilt, but that is the way it is when dealing with the heart. What scared me and tormented my thoughts was the fact that I did not want to create disciples who one day would find themselves as outcasts by the Lord Himself. Here is the passage that has given me and many others trouble and fear in the past.

A good tree cannot bear bad fruit, nor can a bad tree bear good fruit. Every tree that does not bear good fruit is cut down and thrown into the fire. Therefore by their fruits you will know them. **Not everyone who says to Me, "Lord, Lord," shall enter the kingdom of heaven, but he who does the will of My Father in heaven.** *Many will say to Me in that day, "Lord, Lord, have we not prophesied in Your name, cast out demons in Your name, and done many wonders in Your name?" And then I will declare to them, "I never knew you; depart from Me, you who practice lawlessness!"*

Matthew 7:18-23

First we see that Jesus gets done saying that you will know someone by his or her fruit. Then He turns around and says that many who are "bearing fruit" will say "Lord, Lord, let us in Your heaven," but He will tell them to depart for He *never* knew them. This seems absolutely confusing and chilling, to say the least!

Let us now introduce the heart concept here to reconsider the parable. Yes, it is true that your life, or fruit, will be a reflection of what is in your heart. So, you can watch someone's attitude, lifestyle, and words to hear and see what the condition of that person's heart is. What about someone who is working all the power of the Spirit like we are commanded to do in Mark 16? That looks like fruit to me. I know that there are others who deem that as fruit, right? What always terrified me was that I craved to be like Jesus, but in my old mindset this passage gave me no assurance if I would be in heaven or not in the final analysis upon death. It actually used to cause me to shun the very gifts that Paul told me I was to desire, since I did not want to be one of those who only thought they knew Jesus, but in the end proved otherwise!

Jesus said only those who do the will of the Father will enter into the Kingdom of heaven. Consequently, we must ask ourselves, "What is the will of the Father?" It is found in John 6:40: "And this is the will of Him who sent Me, that everyone who sees the Son and believes in Him may have everlasting life; and I will raise him up at the last day." The will of the Father is to believe on Jesus as our righteousness! Let's not be like the Israelites who determined to make their good performances of works their righteousness (Deuteronomy 6:25)!

Notice the people who told Jesus to let them in based on their performance never once said, "But, Jesus, I know You." Those to whom Jesus said, "I don't know you," could point only to the works they were doing and never to the intimacy they had through genuine salvation of the heart. The people Jesus referred to as not knowing Him were those who thought they should inherit heaven based upon their own works. Faith became a work for them. In other words, their fruit was nothing more than a dead work. (I deal with this topic more in depth in another chapter.) Their fruit should have pointed to Jesus; instead, it pointed to their self-performances and self-righteousness. Did not the people Jesus referred to say, "Lord, have we not prophesied in Your name, cast out demons in Your name, and done many wonders in Your name?" They thought that because they worked some miracles, they should earn heaven based upon their own merit. They were transgressors of the law because they came to God apart from the sacrifice of Jesus. They thought they were good enough to deserve heaven. This is why Jesus said, "You who practice lawlessness." Keep in mind that if you have failed in one point of the law, you have failed in it all (James 2:10). No one is righteous without a savior (Romans 3:10).

It is your heart that determines everything! Why do you do what you do? What is your motive? You must examine your heart and keep things pure and simple. Your fruit may look good on the outside to everyone else. Nevertheless, God sees your heart. He sees the true fruit. Doing good things does not mean it is good fruit. It is the power at play behind those works. It is the drive and motive that produces your deeds. Jesus always brought things back to the heart issue.

FIVE WISE AND FIVE FOOLISH: WHICH GROUP WILL YOU BE IN?

As we have looked into the fact that many are born again and going to heaven, yet few enter into the ecstasy of the Kingdom, I wish to lay out a challenge for us as we press forward in this journey. First Timothy 6:19 says, "Storing up for themselves a good foundation for the time to come, that they may lay hold on eternal life." Paul was talking about Christians in this scripture. He was saying that if we do not lay hold of a good foundation, we will not lay hold of the *zoe*, or eternal life, in the time to come. This *zoe* life is the whole package that refers to life today and the life in heaven. He was talking about the Kingdom of God. Man was not made, nor does he have the capacity, to live in fear and pain. God's will is for us to enter His rest and good pleasure. We must be on guard to not forfeit the quality and good life given to us for today and believe only for paradise in heaven. It is this quality of life that Jesus made possible for you and me to enjoy and live. We are not forced to live that quality of life; it is our choice.

Again, in 1 Timothy 6:12 Paul said, "Fight the good fight of faith, *lay hold on eternal life...*" (emphasis added). Paul said to never lose sight of the eternal life, for it is possible to be duped out of our inheritance. The Greek word *sozo*, as discussed in my first book, *How to Release the Power of Faith*, was used when the Bible referred to healing, salvation, prosperity, and deliverance. This *sozo* is the language of the *zoe* at work in the heart and life Jesus modeled and is available for us through Him. In reality, Jesus is both the *sozo* and *zoe*. We are complete in Him.

There is a parable about five wise and five foolish virgins awaiting the bridegroom. I believe there are many lessons within its teaching. I do not believe this was meant to terrify and bring nightmares to the children of God. Instead, I believe it was given to us who persevere in *the* faith of Jesus until the end as a great assurance of our salvation in Him for today and tomorrow. As we begin to grasp the concept of the heart and the Kingdom of God as something for us personally, we can look at this scripture and allow the love of the Father to wash away any doubt and insecurity we may consider about trusting in Jesus alone.

> *Then the kingdom of heaven shall be likened to ten virgins who took their lamps and went out to meet the bridegroom. Now five of them were wise, and five were foolish. Those who were foolish took their lamps and took no oil with them, but the wise took oil in their vessels with their lamps. But while the bridegroom was delayed, they all slumbered and slept. And at midnight a cry was heard: "Behold, the bridegroom is coming; go out to meet him!" Then all those virgins arose and trimmed their lamps. And the foolish said to the wise, "Give us some of your oil, for our lamps are going out." But the wise answered, saying, "No, lest there should not be enough for us and you; but go rather to those who sell, and buy for yourselves." And while they went to buy, the bridegroom came, and those who were ready went in with him to the wedding; and the door was shut. Afterward the other virgins came also, saying, "Lord, Lord, open to us!" But he answered and said, "Assuredly, I say to you, I do not know you."*
>
> Matthew 25:1-12

I truly believe this scripture has as much to do with our life today as it does to our meeting with the Lord in the sky when He comes for us. First the foolish Christians were those who saw no need to trust in the Lord when things were going good in the daytime. Similar to the Laodicean church of Revelation 3:17, many believers don't see a need for Jesus when times are good and finances are in abundance. Howbeit, when the hard times come, those who have not established a relational walk with the Lord perish in the dark hours because of their foolishness during the daytime.

There are two realms of thought I would like to present in this parable. First, if Christians are without oil, which scripturally represents the Holy Spirit, then those Christians are really pretenders. More so, Jesus said that He *never* knew them. This means there was never a time in which the five foolish virgins had a relationship with Jesus as their savior. This then would indicate that the virginity was a false form of godliness. As the Bible says, all who believe on Jesus receive a righteous spirit, which is sealed with the Holy Spirit (Ephesians 1:13). Therefore, all believers have the Holy Spirit (the oil) inside of them once having received Jesus for salvation. Those who *never* were known by Jesus and had no oil (Holy Spirit) would prove that their Christianity was nothing different than any other religion to them. Christianity to those who treat it as a set of rules for moral conduct to earn salvation only are deceiving themselves into believing they have eternal life (John 5:39). They are substituting the free gift of righteousness through faith in Jesus alone with an appearance of religion through laws and good behavior.

Saying there are some Christians who are going to miss the rapture is one viewpoint of this passage. I can guarantee you one thing: God made a promise to never pour His wrath out on us who believe. If Christians are on earth during the years of tribulation, the tribulation is not geared toward the saints. Our covenant with God is based on our representative, who is Jesus. The covenant is between God and Jesus. So it is accurate to say that our covenant is as good as the one representing us, and we are in absolute surety that Jesus is capable of pleasing the Father. Our work and perseverance is to never allow anyone or thing remove us from our faith in Jesus as the basis for our salvation in everything. To pour wrath out on the saints would be double jeopardy. His wrath already was poured out on the body of Jesus, and as saints Jesus took the death on His own body for us. So, if God punished us twice, that would make God unjust. Is God a man that He should lie? Of course not! God would have to apologize to Jesus if He were to pour judgment out on the saints again. Being a saint is not based upon our performance. It is based upon our faith.

*Being a saint is not based upon our performance.
It is based upon our faith.*

All of this is to say that only those who have a true persuasion and an absolute belief and trust in Jesus for their redemption will be the true virgins (born again). Those who know about Jesus, yet trust in their good works to earn salvation, are the virgins who have a form of godliness but deny the true power of its gospel for salvation. Only God knows people's motives and heart beliefs. Although all may appear to believe in Jesus, there are many according to this parable who fool themselves into believing that their outer shell of religion will save them in the last hour. Even more significant is that those who are wise among the born again will know how to get their oil to burn and operate when it is dark.

So, if there are believers on planet Earth during the wrath poured out on those who rejected Jesus, God is not going to pour judgment and wrath on them. They may suffer the pains from the world around them, but it is not God directing wrath on them. In addition, those who believe on Jesus would have access to the limitless power of the Kingdom within them. If some did miss the rapture, or if people believed on Jesus after the saints are taken away, they surely can know that God is not judging them, but the world around them during the years of tribulation.

With that said, and the interpretation "screened" through the three guiding lights, then there is something else we must consider. I believe it is the lost concept of heart and, even further, the lost concept of the Kingdom within. Here is a verse that will help clarify where I am going.

> *Because you have kept My command to persevere, I also will keep you from the hour of trial which shall come upon the whole world, to test those who dwell on the earth.*
>
> Revelation 3:10

Jesus was speaking this to Christians in the church of Philadelphia. In essence, Jesus said that He will keep those who have kept His Word. The word He used when He referred to "keeping" us from the hour of trial was the Greek word *tereo*. This is an awesome word that translates more accurately as to watch over, to guard, or to preserve.[1] So what is the principle that is congruent with all of Scripture? Continue on.

So far we have seen that the Kingdom of God lifestyle is not some external "smear on the forehead" anointing. It is not some quick magic formula to instant gratification. Rather, it is a transformation of life. It is a life based on living from the heart in the state of righteousness. The Kingdom

---

1 James Strong, *The Exhaustive Concordance of the Bible* (Nashville, Tennessee: Holman Bible Publishers, n.d.), #G5083.

is accessed only through the heart. (We will discuss how to access the heart more in Part 2.) What I believe ties these two passages of scripture together is the realm of the Kingdom aspect.

The parable of the five wise and five unwise, is about virgins. But, there was a wisdom aspect that differentiated the two groups. I believe, like in Revelation 3 where Jesus commended the Philadelphian church about their faithfulness, that this also was true about the five wise virgins. They were faithful and were ready with oil in their lamps for the nighttime. Let's face it, folks; we are living in a day of preparation. We as Christians cannot afford to play patty-cake Christianity. There are hard times that lie ahead of us. Why would we wait for a storm to hit before we prepare for it?

We as Christians cannot afford to play patty-cake Christianity.

The five wise virgins were ready for the nighttime. The five foolish had a halfhearted approach, and it wasn't until midnight that they realized they had better get some oil for the darkness that lay ahead. Notice that they did not even think to get the oil (Holy Spirit) to burn a light in the darkness until long after the sun went down. It would appear that they did not believe it would get dark before the bridegroom would arrive. It is not unlike many Christians I meet. They wait for a storm to hit in their life before they attempt to learn the lifestyle and freedom of the Kingdom given through Jesus. One problem with that mindset is that the Kingdom is something you already must be established in when the time of trouble hits if it is to be of any value.

For example, if you are in a state of health and a disease attacks your body, you may change an eating habit or some other external measure to correct a potential abuse to your body. However, by starting out in a state of health as provided by Jesus, you will not switch over to fearful emotions and feelings; rather, you will remain calm and at peace knowing the disease cannot have control and final verdict. If a disease struck your body and you were not established in a state of health, then you would struggle *trying* to get healed and chase healing as a *goal rather than a state of being.*

The same is true with any of the promises and inheritance you have through

Jesus' finished work. You can view prosperity the same way. If you were facing poverty externally, but lived in a state of prosperity internally, the poverty would not have influence over you. You then would be greater than your circumstance. You would still feel and experience the emotions of prosperity in the midst of ruin. It would be impossible to remain in the midst of poverty when abiding in and experiencing prosperity within. Poverty would not have rule over you; you would be in position of clarity for God to reveal the opportunities and potential all around beyond the temporary impoverished circumstance. You can see this epic example with Joseph and his brothers!

Like the foolish virgins in the parable, you cannot try to buy the Kingdom of God. It is learned through the heart of the individual. I truly believe in these last days that there will be Christians living supernaturally while others will be floundering in frustration. The unprepared will see the prepared flourishing. They will try to enter that Kingdom life at the last moment, but it is something learned and practiced more than instantly downloaded. Many people are not willing to enter the realm of the heart. There are countless Christians who only will believe something if they can first understand it. They prefer to empower logical theology and their endless arguments than learning practical living from the heart. But, isn't that the purpose of the Word—to lead us into a life and vibrant relationship with our Father? And how is that life discovered and walked out? Look no further than the Kingdom within you, through the doorway of the heart. Many would rather talk than walk in power in utter surrender to the unction of the Holy Spirit. To live out of the heart is very intimidating and scary for the logical and religious mind. Many will never be able to surrender to that simplicity.

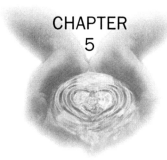

THE PURPOSE OF
PARABLES

*J*esus taught in a way that if you had a heart for His message you would catch it; and if you did not, then you wouldn't. Jesus made a certain statement in Mark chapter 4—Matthew recorded the same in Matthew 13—that was absolutely confusing to say the least when I first laid eyes on it. I was amazed He would say something that seemed so contrary to the whole purpose of why He came to Earth as a man. The more I gave time to studying it, the more it really used to bother me. I was even a little irritated that He would not plainly tell me in the Gospels what I so dearly wanted to learn. After all, I was a follower of His, yet He spoke in riddles that held the secret to who He is and the power He walked in. What was most irritating was that, in my immaturity, I was upset at how unfair it was that the disciples could talk to Jesus in the flesh, whereas I was left with letters to interpret on my own with the Holy Spirit. I know, that is a pretty low thing to feel about the Comforter, but like I said, I was immature.

And the disciples came and said to Him, "Why do You speak to them in parables?" He answered and said to them, "Because it has been given to you to know the mysteries of the kingdom of heaven, but to them it has not been given. For whoever has, to him more will be given, and he will have abundance; but whoever does not have, even what he has will be taken away from him. Therefore I speak to them in parables, because seeing they do not see, and hearing they do not hear, nor do they understand. And in them the prophecy of Isaiah is fulfilled, which says: 'Hearing you will hear and shall not understand, and seeing you will see and not perceive; for the hearts of this people have grown dull. Their ears are hard of hearing, and their eyes they have closed, lest they should see with their eyes and hear with their ears, lest they should understand with their hearts and turn, so that I should heal them.'"

Matthew 13:10-15

I did not realize it for some time, but this scripture passage is often what atheists use to try and debunk the Bible as an unreliable source. Jesus claimed to come to save, heal, and reach people, but these verses report what appears to be quite the opposite of Jesus' feelings when alone with His disciples. Truly, it gives me such joy to write this chapter, as I am sure there are others who will be set free and see Jesus' logic in quite a new light apart from what our religious mind have portrayed.

JUSTIFICATION OF EGO

I am going to have to lay a little groundwork before I can wrap up in simplicity what Jesus was revealing in Matthew 13:10-15. First, I have to point out the fact that many people come to God or read His Word with merely the purpose to justify themselves. Those people may have some selfish ambition, some attitude, or even a desire to defend some action they are doing. So they go to the Word and look for a verse to justify their actions or attitude. Humans have this insatiable need to be right. Often, in our human wisdom, we try to appease our conscience by getting some spiritual guidance to pet our pride. This is exactly what happened with a lawyer in Luke 10.

And behold, a certain lawyer stood up and tested Him, saying, "Teacher, what shall I do to inherit eternal life?" He said to him, "What is written *in the law? What is your reading of it?" So he answered and said, "'You shall love the LORD your God with all your heart, with all your soul, with all your strength, and with all your mind,' and 'your neighbor as yourself.'" And He said to him, "You have answered rightly; do this and you will live." **But he, wanting to justify himself, said to Jesus, "And who is my neighbor?"***

Luke 10:25-29, emphasis added

Isn't that amazing! Jesus was able to pull out the true motive of this lawyer. First, Jesus asked this lawyer what was written and how he interpreted it. *That right there is what we need to ask ourselves. What do we read, and why do we interpret it the way we do?* Those questions are a great test to find out what our motives are and see what is established in our hearts.

Within moments we see the response of the lawyer: "Who is my neighbor?" Out of his own mouth he revealed his purpose. The Word says it was because he wanted to justify himself. This lawyer did not want to love everyone. He wanted to do just enough to get by. So, if Jesus would say whoever lives next door to you, then that he could do. But, in classic Jesus style, Jesus took it to a level very few Jews could fathom. He made the point that the neighbor was anyone near you, including the Samaritan.

The lawyer in this story was not receiving freedom. He couldn't. His heart was not open to God with sincerity; he had ulterior motives. The moral here is that you only experience freedom to the degree you are willing to deal with your issues.

Hold all of these little scripture passages in mind, for I will use these to bring together the final thought of why Jesus used parables. Next, I want to look at an example of the disciples' hardened hearts and what effect it had on their understanding.

SPIRITUALLY DISABLED

Then He charged them, saying, "Take heed, beware of the leaven of the Pharisees and the leaven of Herod." And they reasoned among themselves, saying, "It is because we have no bread." But Jesus, being aware of *it, said to them, "Why do you reason because you have no bread? **Do you not yet perceive nor understand? Is your heart still hardened? Having eyes, do you not see? And having ears, do you not hear? And do you not remember?** When I broke the five loaves for the five thousand, how many baskets full of fragments did you take up?" They said to Him, "Twelve."*

Mark 8:15-19, emphasis added

When Jesus started to talk to the disciples about the leaven, or doctrine, of the Pharisees, the disciples felt guilty because they did not have any food with them. They thought Jesus was giving them the guilt trip in a roundabout way for not having food. It was such an absurd thought for these disciples when considering whom they were traveling with, as Jesus pointed out. Jesus went on to make it very clear that the last thing He was worried about was food. He had to remind them of the five thousand and later the four thousand who were fed by His multiplying food miraculously.

You only experience freedom to the degree you are willing to deal with your issues.

What I really wanted to point out, however, is what Jesus dealt with directly was a hardened heart. When someone's heart is hard, you see that the individual loses his or her ability to perceive and understand. In addition to losing perception and understanding, the person also does not remember. When Jesus said, "Do you have eyes and not see?" He was talking about the eyes of the heart that perceive. When He referred to having ears to hear and not hear, He was referring to understanding what they heard. One of the most common ways hardness of heart toward God begins is by unbelief and distraction. Whatever we place our focus and regard on is what our heart will be soft toward. The disciples were merely placing their attention on outside circumstances more than esteeming the One who was with them. If people's heart is hard, they can encounter God all day long but never grasp His person in their hearts. They will never understand the depths and rapture of the moment due to a hardened heart. It is as if they are spiritually insensitive or debilitated.

Having a hardened heart does not mean you are a bad person. It just means your focus and purpose is on something else outside of God. As Andrew Wommack says, "The disciples were not in the bottom of the boat looking at pornography."[1] They simply were not esteeming the miracle that they witnessed with the loaves and fishes. Therefore, they forgot and dismissed it from their daily walk with the Lord. Had they esteemed the work of Jesus, they would have known He would not worry about food in the first place. It is so important that you remember the testimonies and miracles of God in your life!

We know that all true understanding and wisdom comes from the heart, not the logical mind. Jesus understood this better than anyone. He also knew that once someone truly believed, he or she then could perceive. In addition, understanding in the heart only comes by believing first. Perceiving through the eyes of the heart is only for those who believe first, just like spiritual understanding. When someone does not believe, it is like closing the eyes of the heart.

UNDERSTANDING BY FAITH

Hebrews makes an awesome statement about understanding by faith. Hebrews 11:3 says, "By faith we understand that the worlds were framed by the word of God...." It is by faith that we understand. It really is not much simpler than that. You can have all of the logical understanding in the world, yet you will never scrape the surface of understanding the spiritual realities with logic alone.

It is very similar to children. Jesus said you have to become like a child if you want to enter the Kingdom of God. So too is it with understanding. Suppose you have a five- or six-year-old who wants to know how something works in your home, such as the water from the faucet. If you live in the country, you explain that the water comes from under the ground through a well and, powered by electricity, a pump brings it into the house and in through the kitchen faucet. The child really does not comprehend what you are saying, but still says, "Okay," and often that is enough. The child believes you; that is the way it is for children.

---

1 Andrew Wommack, "Hardness of Heart," audio teaching series.

Wouldn't it be ridiculous if the six-year-old said, "That cannot be true because I don't understand it!" That is exactly what many of us Christians do with God. A six-year-old believes it, then with time as their mind grows and learns, they can comprehend how all the mechanics work. That is the same with God and us. I don't understand everything before I believe it. I believe Him; then as I grow with time, I begin to understand the concepts, spiritual laws, and principles at work. I would be one of the stupidest people on earth to say to God, "Unless I can understand what You are telling me, then I won't believe." That would mean I was limiting God to functioning only within the confines of my peanut brain.

First we believe, then we understand. It is not the other way around! I am so happy that it is not the other way around. Life would get boring awfully quickly if it were limited to my capacity of understanding. I have an eternity of learning and growing in Him. My eternity is exciting, and I look forward to every day.

First we believe, then we understand.

If you are training people to understand so that they can believe, I want to tell you that that approach is completely unbiblical. You must train people to understand what they already believe. Understanding does not bring you to a place of believing. Believing, however, leads you to a place of true understanding. In Mark 4:19 Jesus said that Satan steals the Word immediately out of your heart when you don't understand. This is why it is critical to learn from children that you do not need to understand prior to believing, but rather your believing is crucial for the groundwork of understanding to take place. If you and I approach the Lord with a pure believing heart, the words He speaks will be made into simple understanding for us, which does not require complicated explanation. It is then that the enemy cannot steal the Word, for you had simple belief and consequently understood.

Purity of heart is a state of being. It is the purity that Jesus is Lord and that we choose to believe what and where He leads us. It is like a child knowing that the parent has his or her best interest in mind and can fully trust to a point of no worry. The purity of heart is a state of being where one is not on guard to defend personal opinions or traditions. It is a state where one is continuously yielded to grow in the knowledge and grace of Jesus.

Again, I must reiterate that when I talk about believing, I am not talking about intellectual facts! Believing in the manner of the heart changes the entire thinking process of your mind. This believing is so deeply rooted in you that your reality actually revolves around the unyielding belief of your heart. Biblical belief here is worlds apart from the academic belief of historical or theoretical facts. The belief I speak of changes one's paradigm even deep inside the subconscious.

Let's wrap up here with two verses to tie these all together. Job 38:36 says, "Who hath put wisdom in the inward parts? or who hath given understanding to the heart?" (KJV) The wisdom of God and understanding are within the heart! They are not a product of our intellect. That is how the wisdom of God is able to confound the wise of the world. The world relies on logic. We, however, rely on God's wisdom through the heart. We have something that logic cannot know, for logic is based upon proof. The wisdom of God is based upon faith. That wisdom is accessed through the heart.

To quickly interpose, there are some of you who may be asking a few questions about the logical mind not being able to know faith. There is a reference in Acts 17:11 that speaks of the Bereans being more noble than the Thessalonicans because they received the Word with willingness of mind and daily searched the Scriptures to see whether what they heard was so. Notice that the Bereans first were willing to believe wholeheartedly. Then, they searched the prophecies to see if what they were told about Jesus was true. That is wisdom. It is a perfect balance of the natural and spiritual harmonizing together. They knew in their hearts that God was speaking through Paul and Silas, yet they confirmed the word given by these men through the written prophecies. Once the truth about Jesus was confirmed in the Scriptures, the Bereans were able to fully surrender to a life of faith, living from the heart guided by the Spirit of Christ, which would never contradict His own Word.

David makes an incredible statement in Psalm 49:3-4: "My mouth shall speak of wisdom; and the meditation of my heart shall be of understanding. I will incline mine ear to a parable..." (KJV). He says that his mouth will speak wisdom. Out of the abundance of the heart the mouth speaks, right? He also has set his heart to meditate on understanding. This would mean that meditating on understanding would cause us to speak wisdom. Then David said he looks for parables to hear and give his attention to. That is a statement from someone who is pliable and teachable. Here is a mark of someone who is growing and increasing in understanding, someone who is not lazy in his own heart.

Now, let's sum all of this up to understand why Jesus used parables.

THE CONSENSUS

And when he was alone, they that were about him with the twelve asked of him the parable. And he said unto them, Unto you it is given to know the mystery of the kingdom of God: but unto them that are without, all these things are done in parables: that seeing they may see, and not perceive; and hearing they may hear, and not understand; lest at any time they should be converted, and their sins should be forgiven them.

Mark 4:10-12 KJV

Taking a look in Mark's account of "the parable," we find our first clues. The first hint is found in the fact that those who were with Him alone sought to understand the parable. Just like David said in Psalm 49:4, "I will incline mine ear to a parable" (KJV), those who were with Jesus were *inclining* their ears—the ears of their heart. This is similar to Moses and the children of Israel. The Bible records that the Israelites saw God's mighty works, whereas Moses not only saw but also understood God's ways. My choice is to be like Moses. I don't want to see only; I also want to understand and perceive God, His heart, and logic. Howbeit, God leaves that for us to choose and discover. Remember, Jesus perceives; Pharisees reason.

Jesus then said that to those who were inclining their ears it was given to know the mystery of the Kingdom of God. But, He said, for those who are on the outside, all things come in parables. This is the second clue. Who is on the outside? The outsiders are those who are entering solely through their logic and reasoning. Those who are on the "inside" are those who have entered into the realm of faith, the realm of heart. Notice that those who

questioned Jesus here were not like the scribes and Pharisees who only studied and worked during business hours. These people lived the message and
craved to walk further with Jesus. These believers were still meditating and
pondering the message and truth after everyone else left and went home.

Next, Jesus says, "That seeing they may see, and not perceive; and hearing
they may hear, and not understand; lest at any time they should be converted,
and their sins should be forgiven them." This can be quite a mouthful. To me
this particular statement was a mindbender for more than ten years.

We must remember as we look at this that without faith it is impossible to please God. In fact, anything that is not of faith is sin! So, let's ask
ourselves this question: "Why would God encourage people to come to Him
apart from faith?" It is by grace we have been saved through faith (Ephesians
2:8-9). So, how is someone supposed to access grace without faith?

Jesus understood these things better than anyone. After all, He is the
author of faith. Have you ever noticed that our methods of seeking out the
lost and begging them to pray a sinner's prayer with us are drastically different than Jesus' approach? Jesus was not insecure by any means. He did not get
His approval ratings based upon numbers. Jesus was after a person's heart. If
the person was not ready to give it, He did not force the issue by debating and
using arguments. Jesus never convinced someone to pray a prayer he or she did
not mean from the heart. He said that if we are ashamed of Him before men,
then He is ashamed of us before His Father. Don't take me wrong; Jesus loved
the world so much that He gave His life to be butchered on a cross for all of
mankind. It is our free choice now as to whether we will receive, with the purpose of applying, His sacrifice and the righteousness He freely gave to our lives.

Continuing on with the passage of seeing, perceiving, hearing, and understanding, we can finish this up by zeroing in on the heart. To begin with, Jesus
used parables so that people would see the miracles and hear the teachings,
but it was like a failsafe method of teaching so that only those with passion
and willingness of heart could reach the depths of spiritual understanding.
To those who only came around Jesus for the benefits and those who were
there only to criticize, the parables were nothing more than moral stories.
Parables are a way of teaching that does not allow God to bring anything
in our life until *we* are ready to release *our* current perception. Like a double

meaning picture, it appears to be one thing, but with a little study and diligence another image emerges into something totally different.

> *And in them the prophecy of Isaiah is fulfilled, which says: "Hearing you will hear and shall not understand, and seeing you will see and not perceive; for the hearts of this people have grown dull. Their ears are hard of hearing, **and their eyes they have closed**, lest they should see with their eyes and hear with their ears, lest they should understand with their hearts and turn, so that I should heal them."*
>
> Matthew 13:14-15 KJV, emphasis added

Isaiah even prophesied that Jesus would use parables so that those who had closed their hearts would not see or understand. Ultimately, Jesus wanted to heal everyone. But, just like the rejection He received from His hometown and therefore could not heal more than a few, so too was Jesus limited to as many as would receive Him. The parable is a beautiful way of teaching. For the teacher who wants the students to grow the most, one cannot be insecure. He or she must see that, when teaching in quality over quantity, it will take time to cultivate the disciple. There is no overnight formula. At the same time, without the passion of the student, a teacher is very limited.

Proverbs 25:2 says that it is the glory of God to conceal a matter, but it is the glory of kings to reveal it. You and I are called kings and priests through the position Christ restored to us. That's why the Bible says that Jesus is King of kings and Lord of lords, referring to us. According to the Scriptures, if we seek the Lord with all our hearts, then we will find Him. Parables are a grand way for us to seek and discover. If we do not seek, then the parable will remain superficial. The parable is satisfying to the seeker and non-seeker alike. The seeker gets to unravel the mystery and its many lessons within, and the non-seeker gets his feel-good superficial gratification.

WHAT MEASURE?

> *Then He said to them, "Take heed what you hear. With the same measure you use, it will be measured to you; and to you who hear, more will be*

given. For whoever has, to him more will be given; but whoever does not have, even what he has will be taken away from him."

Mark 4:24-25

Jesus spoke this shortly after giving the parable of the sower and the seed. We often hear this phrase and we somehow assume that God is the One who will give or take away. That is never once implied. In fact, Job in his useless and arrogant ramblings made that statement, which God later rebuked him for. It is our responsibility to be aware and regard what we hear. To the same degree you give attention to and apply yourself, that is the very degree of learning, understanding, and value you will get back out of a matter. This passage says to him who has, more will be given. This indicates that what knowledge and understanding we already have, as we continue to hear and apply ourselves, we will learn and grow in addition to what we already have working inside of us. Howbeit, to the person who does not have, (that is, understanding), as that person continues to not hear, apply him or herself, and remain opinionated and sluggish in faith, even what little knowledge and understanding he or she has will be lost and that person will go backwards in that area of life.

We never live in neutral. Either we are growing or we are dying. No one just simply stays in one place. The ancient Apache had a saying that went like this: "The day you stop learning is the day you start dying." Again, in Proverbs 18:9 in the Amplified Bible, it says that someone who is lazy is "brother to him who commits suicide." The point here is that no one just exists. Either we are moving forward, or we are moving backwards. A lazy person is just living out a very slow suicidal death.

Perceiving is opening your eyes through your heart. Perceiving also is like using another sense beyond your five physical senses. It is like you know you know, but you don't know how you know. It is that intimate part of you that reaches deeper than physical logic. The understanding that Jesus referred to here was not about logical understanding in a mathematical sense. This understanding goes well beyond. It makes sense within your heart. Understanding here adds up the "math" in spiritual matters of faith, much like the logical mind works to analyze physical matters and appropriate the tangible world with the evidence of proof. When your heart is properly established, your spiritual understanding will begin to find and see good all around you, in any situation (Proverbs 17:20).

Perceiving is opening your eyes through your heart.

The spiritual understanding Jesus is talking about does not need proof like the logical mind. The only proof spiritual understanding needs is the fact that Jesus spoke it. If Jesus said it, then it is true, and it is now your job to believe it. From there the understanding will be made manifest. The understanding will make the connections of what you know and believe to the relevance of life's current scenario. You can enter the Kingdom only if you come like little children and only believe.

Let's finish up with what Jesus said about "lest they should turn, and their sins be forgiven them." Jesus did not want to persuade people to believe on Him based upon their logical reasoning alone, through some argument. He wanted a people who came to Him because they chose to open their eyes and simply believe. You see, if you win people to the Lord through their intellect alone, you are setting them up for possible failure. They will use their reason and arguments to maintain their walk with the Lord. The only problem here is, if someone comes with some other "gospel" of persuasive words different than faith righteousness in Jesus, they will be likely to sway over to an argument that externally sounds better than what they knew from you. The physical approach to spiritual matters can never work. Either people believe or they don't. You cannot force someone into softening his or her heart. That is something people must choose to do on their own. You can love them and walk with them, being an example that God could use to work on them, but you can never trick someone into believing from the heart.

CHAPTER 6

WHEAT & TARES

*D*iscovering that parables are understood when you grasp that they all deal with the heart of a person and not some methodology is a huge step in the right direction. I want to take you on a short journey into one such parable that I believe will greatly give you a head start. In regards to parables, Jesus said that the parable of the sower and the seed was a key to understanding all the parables. The key was the heart. All of Jesus' parables were about the heart in relationship to righteousness and the Kingdom of God.

Jesus referred to the Kingdom of God in so many parables, but we understood that to mean going to heaven when we die. Jesus wanted *today* to be our day of salvation (2 Corinthians 6:2). He wanted us to have and live eternal life the moment we believed on Him. Why have we shrugged it off as "some pie in the sky I'll have in that sweet bye and bye"? Today is our day. When I began to understand this key to parables, my eyes opened to a completely new level of reading the stories Jesus told. Furthermore, this concept of salvation after we die is only a westernized idea. The people Jesus ministered to in His day believed in salvation for the here and now.

All throughout the Old Covenant we see references about blessings and cursing for life on earth. These people thought in present-tense realities.

GOOD SEED AND BAD SEED

Another parable He put forth to them, saying: "The kingdom of heaven is like a man who sowed good seed in his field; but while men slept, his enemy came and sowed tares among the wheat and went his way. But when the grain had sprouted and produced a crop, then the tares also appeared. So the servants of the owner came and said to him, 'Sir, did you not sow good seed in your field? How then does it have tares?' He said to them, 'An enemy has done this.' The servants said to him, 'Do you want us then to go and gather them up?' But he said, 'No, lest while you gather up the tares you also uproot the wheat with them. Let both grow together until the harvest, and at the time of harvest I will say to the reapers, "First gather together the tares and bind them in bundles to burn them, but gather the wheat into my barn."'"

Matthew 13:24-30

I don't believe it is any coincidence that this parable comes immediately after the parable of the sower and the seed in Matthew. One of the main applications of this story is the enemy coming at night while men slept. An example of this would be deception coming from the philosophies and lies that are mixed into a truth that we listen to and embrace—all the while unaware of how it is affecting our heart. The deception from within always causes greater destruction than an external opposing force working against us.

Let's examine this parable in the application of the heart. First, Jesus was talking about the Kingdom of heaven. Remember, the Kingdom of God and the Kingdom of heaven refer to a realm and a provision of that realm. There were occasions when Jesus specifically spoke of the Kingdom of heaven in reference to the third heaven alone, or the place where we go after we die. But, more often than not, He spoke of the Kingdom as something we experience and live here on planet Earth. I believe that this passage has application to the third heaven at the end of the age. But, I also believe the truth of this passage has some great insight into our own personal lives.

In verse 25 the parable says that as men slept the enemy came to sow tares among the wheat. Looking at 1Thessalonians 5:6-8, we are commanded not to sleep as others do. We are commanded to be aware and sober-minded. Sober-minded means to not have our mind or emotions influenced in a way that alters our perception outside of the life of God. For example, if I am given to anger often, then when I have those fits of rage my perception of the world will change to view everything through lenses of anger and rage. (As a brief side note, I will point out that the Bible speaks volumes more about emotional drunkenness than it does about drunkenness with alcohol!) If we are looking through the lenses of anger, fear, worry, greed, lust, lack, or the like, then we are operating in an altered state of consciousness. We see life through those rose-colored glasses, so to speak, and miss the purity and reality of things as they truly are.

Consequently, in this parable the enemy was able to sow bad seed in the field only while men slept. One more thing to point out: the field. The field in the parable just before of the sower and seed represented the heart. The seed from the parable before characterized the Word. We know that faith comes by hearing. Guess what? Fear also enters the heart by hearing.

Bad seed was planted in the field. Or you could say, bad word was planted in the soil of the heart while men were unaware or inattentive. When the Word of God is planted, what are we supposed to do with it? We believe it and allow it to transform us by the belief and value we give to the Word. However, not all words are good. There are also seeds that are contrary to the seed of the Word of God. We further need to recognize what a tare is. A tare is a plant that grows in with wheat that is difficult to identify separate from the wheat in the growing stages, but the fruit is when you really see the difference. Tares have tiny little seeds that do not yield much at all. If mixed with wheat in harvest, you get a crop of seeds for the next year that can ruin an entire field and overrun the wheat, destroying the good crop.

Whatever we establish our heart on is what we focus on in life. So, whatever word we allow into our heart beliefs, that is what will determine how we will view the life around us even on a subconscious level. The deceptiveness of a tare when sown in our heart while we are unaware is that it alters our beliefs, but we don't always consciously know how our beliefs got out of line with God's. Many times we don't even know we stepped out of line with the life of God until we see attitudes, imaginations, fears, thoughts, and the sense of lack grow strong enough to where we catch ourselves responding to life according to the sometimes slightly skewed beliefs we adopted while totally unaware.

Many times I have noticed in my own life attitudes that get off track or wrong through patterns. When I take a moment to examine my heart as to why things are affecting me negatively, I find that "tares" got into my heart. Sometimes I am amazed at what I find working in my heart! I even am amazed as to how those things got there. Once identified, however, I can deal with the issues and send them away, then rewrite and establish the truth in their place.

*Whatever we establish our heart on
is what we focus on in life.*

Remember that the heart is like the control center to your entire being. It is the core of your absolute belief system. Those beliefs control and determine the course of your entire life and the quality thereof. With this said, see that the owner of the field had wisdom to tell his servants not to gather up the tares until the harvest season. The concern there was that they would destroy the good plants if they tried to gather the bad prior to examining the fruit they bore.

THE SEED-WORD

Now, look at the seed as the Word. Jesus said those who receive His Word in their hearts would receive a harvest—some thirty-, some sixty-, and some a hundred-fold yield. What does that mean? When the Word of God is adopted in your belief system, that Word will begin to grow and transform you at a heart level. Once your heart transforms, so too will your thoughts, feelings, and emotions. Thus, it births what was spirit into a manifestation in the physical. To the degree you give yourself to the Word, that is the degree of crop you yield in return. You cannot live contrary to the way you believe. So, too, do people with faulty beliefs bear fruit. Their fruit is death, corruption, and chaos. Anyone attempting to live and find truth apart from the principles and laws of God will never operate in a capacity of fulfillment and life. The best thing the enemy, Satan, could do is to give you half-truths. A wonderful tactic is to get you focused on physical realities over the realities of the spirit and truth. When you do that, you grow bad fruit from your heart.

Take a look at Cain's example of being marked by God after killing Abel. God extended mercy to Cain and did not hold his sin against him. So, a short time later Lamech killed a man in self-defense and boasted that God should justify and extend greater mercy toward him. His carnal logic was polluting his heart by comparing one man's outward appearance with his own. This is an example of our believing half-truths to pursue our own logic over seeking the Father's heart. Eventually, the whole world began to compare and think that God only winked at sin and justified their actions based upon comparing themselves to one another. This deceitful and carnal theology plagued the world until all had walked away from the Lord completely, except for Noah as the last righteous man on earth. "There is a way that seems right to a man, but its end is the way of death" (Proverbs 14:12).

The reason we wait until a harvest to check the beliefs or word that was planted in our heart is so we can identify and know what the bad seed is apart from the good seed we have been planting. We as human beings generally do not deal with our issues until pain is involved. When we can see the chaos and pain, which "our way" brings, then those are the times we tend to deal with it. Unfortunately, some people require more pain in their lives than others to bring about a change of heart. Our way of doing things outside of God, such as work, traditions, culture, opinions, and even our experiences, do not and cannot bring life to a close grade of what Jesus brings. Once we fully can see the error of our beliefs, we can then gather them up, replace them with the truth of God's Word, and burn away the old way of life.

We wait until a harvest to check the beliefs or word that was planted in our heart so we can identify and know what the bad seed is apart from the good seed we have been planting.

A quick story of what I just recently witnessed that was a perfect harmony of this parable is from a recent evangelistic trip I had to the Dominican Republic. My friend and I were on an airplane headed to the Dominican to work with a church and the surrounding community. We talked for hours about the Word and things God had been doing and sharing with us. I remember about an hour into the plane ride that my friend laid his head back and began to drift to sleep. I then remembered being surprised at the quick change in attitude, but passed it off as his gathering the much-needed rest for the adventure ahead.

The next day we were talking privately in the time we had to ourselves, and he began to tell me what was going on within him from the day before. He said to start with he had a phone message from a close friend warning him about the H1N1 flu hype and how in airports he could get infected quite easily. He relayed how strange it was for his friend to go on and on with concern, even suggesting that he wear a mask and gloves. Understanding the principles of sowing good and bad seed into the heart, he felt these words affect him emotionally and so started building a defense against these words. After a while, he said, he began to speak to the voice mail, "*No*, it's a lie; I have life! *No!*" Then he deleted the message.

Throughout that day and the next the memory of the phone call came back to him. A battle waged in his mind. Fear would seep in and he would think, *What if it does happen? What if I do get attacked by the H1N1?* And then, *No, I am not going to let those words take root. I rebuke those thoughts in Jesus' name!* He kept trying to push back those thoughts and divert his thinking to something else. Finally, at the moment on the plane we were talking about earlier, he started to feel feverish. His neck glands started to swell. He began having the sensation that he wanted to throw up. He then realized that what he had been doing over the past two days had not been working. He had to do something else. That was when he laid his head back and got quiet. He started to turn his thoughts toward the finished work of Jesus; he began to rest in his relationship with a kind and loving Father who only wanted the best for him. By the time we touched down, most of the symptoms he was experiencing were gone—and he walked off the plane with victory in his body.

What happened on the plane was that those words tried to take root in his core. He said on the plane he began to feel unusual. Pressure was building in his head; his throat ached, and he didn't feel himself. He knew this was directly from the words spoken into him the day before, when fear tried to enter by the memory of the phone message. At that time he laid his head back and resisted the symptoms within and by intent pushed them out. After a couple hours of that he recovered!

I was so excited to hear this in remembering the parable of the wheat and tares! Let me explain. Most of us would see the tares as growing from the seed planted in the words of the voicemail. But, when we take a closer look, the seed from the voicemail as took root and grew didn't look like wheat at all. The true tare was the way he focused on and trusted in the words of the voicemail message. I am not saying that we don't take action against a bad word spoken into our life; rather, how do we approach it initially? My friend admitted that fear came in as he was listening to the voicemail. It was not actually fear of the virus but fear of the power of the words. Then, as he fought against it by shouting at the phone and later rebuking the returning thoughts, he actually was giving them substance and validity. It seemed like the right thing to do at the time, but eventually he was able to see its fruit. At that point he realized that his focus was misdirected and he turned his focus back onto the finished work of Jesus. He rested on the love and promises of God, and there he brought himself to a place of peaceful trust. Without anything left to feed on, the bad word from the voicemail finally died. The shift from one focal point to another can be so slight. That's why it is so hard to tell if it's wheat or tares in the beginning. Once it starts bearing fruit, it becomes more obvious which is which. My friend told me if he had not been aware and on guard, there is no doubt he would have been sick the entire trip. He was not "asleep" in regards to his heart. He recognized what was happening and resisted the foul word by looking unto Jesus. That which kills us is that which we are not aware of. *"The words of the wicked are to lie in wait for blood*: but the mouth of the upright shall deliver them" (Proverbs 12:6 KJV, emphasis added).

CHAPTER 7

CORINTHIAN & GALATIAN CHURCHES

*T*here are two churches for which the apostle Paul used two quite different approaches to correcting error in their church bodies. His approaches have absolutely everything to do with the heart. We have much to learn from his stance on dealing with errors in the church. The churches I am referring to are the church of Corinth and the church of Galatia. These two approaches are great examples to us of how we should deal with one another when someone has fallen from grace or if someone has become carnal in his or her spirituality. I believe that this chapter will really help communicate to us this area of the heart.

Recently I had a mother of a twenty-one-year-old son ask me for help to lead this young man to the Lord Jesus. I told her that he already had confessed Jesus as his Lord and Savior, but she denied the legitimacy due to his lifestyle of sin. Now, before I continue on, I will once again repeat myself and say that I do not condone sin, nor do I promote stupidity in people's lives. Because I personally knew the sincerity of the young man's heart and his situation, I was able to say what I am about to share. This man very much desired to walk with the Lord; he just lacked the guidance. His upbringing was not that great; neither did he have any real role models who exemplified a genuine love. To be quite honest, he was given everything he wanted when he wanted it since a baby. He was never taught disciplines or structure as to simple laws of sowing and reaping. He was spoiled, to say the least.

To continue on, I was able to assess the situation as one of a mother trained in a religion that told her that unless someone lives a "perfect" and "holy," morally perfected life, then that person's born-again experience was not valid. It was then that I relayed this example of the Corinthian and Galatian approaches used by the apostle Paul.

A TALE OF TWO CHURCHES

The church of Corinth was a church that had all kinds of weird things going on. They would get drunk at communion. Not only that, but they would feast and gorge themselves on the bread instead of honoring the Lord Jesus. They were a church of people who had come away from worshipping in the temples of pagan gods, which included having priestesses with whom they would have orgies. When Paul wrote his first letter to them, they were still practicing some of these things in the church gatherings! The Corinthian church had one messed-up background, much like many of us before we found the Lord.

Paul preached Jesus to these people, and they believed. Never do we find Paul coming in a new region and preaching the Ten Commandments! He preached righteousness by faith in Jesus Christ. In fact, Paul said that we are no longer under the ministry of death and condemnation, but rather under the ministry of righteousness! He preached that good news of God sending His Son so that we as mankind can be sons and daughters again in His Kingdom without fear of judgment. We are His offspring and have been restored to our rightful position. Paul preached the power of the gospel, which is the grace of Jesus Christ. These people received Jesus, but they still carried some of their pagan baggage with them. Paul knew he did not have to come in with harsh commandments and legalism to clean these believers up. He simply knew the power of the gospel! Once people fall in love with Jesus, they will naturally transform into His image (1 John 3:3). The Corinthians were just ignorant and unaware of their true identity. It was education they needed.

Now, on the other hand, let me give you a quick review of the Galatian church before we dive into the heart of this subject. The Galatian church also received the good news of Jesus with sincerity. It was after Paul left the church plant of Galatia that Judaizers followed behind him and mixed their doctrine in with the gospel that Paul preached. Judaizers believed that Jesus was the savior, but they also believed that in order to stay saved and keep God happy with you, you had to continue to fulfill the Torah law as given by Moses. To sum it up more clearly, they believed that Jesus was the down payment for your salvation, but you had to keep making the monthly installments through good behavior to remain saved.

I know this is a very absurd teaching and does not mathematically add up, but isn't that the formula for religion? Insanity! Either Jesus did a complete work on the cross, or He didn't. Either He was a perfect sacrifice to come to the throne of God with, or He was not. Let's just call it for what it is. Well, these Judaizers came and told the Galatians in their simple faith that they now had to add circumcision to their believing on Jesus. This teaching grew popular, and the Galatians fell for it. They began to embrace this action, or law, with their faith. Therefore, as Paul so perfectly put it, they fell from grace (Galatians 5:4)! I know, most people think falling from grace is sinning. Actually, falling from grace is when you remove yourself from the covenant God made for mankind through the grace of Jesus, and instead believe upon your own performance and righteousness to save you.

One of these two churches Paul rebuked; the other he encouraged and reminded the people of their identity in Christ and who they were as sanctified saints. This I ask you: Which people group would you have rebuked, and on which would you have focused establishing their identity?

If you were anything like me, you would have rebuked the carnal Christian for walking in sin and reminded the legalistic Christian of his or her true identity. Well, that is the exact opposite of what the apostle Paul did! He took the carnal Christian, living in all kinds of stupid, sinful acts, and called them sanctified, saints, righteous, and so on. He then focused on telling them that the way they were living was contrary to who they truly were in the spirit of Christ. He reminded them how they were the temple of God. Going on to say to this motley crew that their salvation and security were God's doing, he expressed his confidence in them and in God's finishing what He started. Paul was very encouraging in reinforcing their identity as a people of hope and that they were secure in God!

It was the Galatian church that Paul had the rebuke for. When Paul addressed the Galatians, he was not soft by any means. He used a word to describe their state of mind as being "bewitched." This Greek word for "bewitched" was the only time it was ever used in the New Testament, and it is one of the strongest words in the Bible to describe demonic activity! Paul asked them why they thought they could be saved by grace in the spirit, but then somehow have to earn it by adding a law to faith. He strongly condemned these new beliefs that were what he called "another gospel." Any gospel apart from the grace of our Lord is another gospel, and even more accurately put, a doctrine of demons. Paul said that any person or angel that preaches any other gospel than the simplicity of faith in Jesus Christ is to be accursed.

The reason I had to go into this example of the two churches was to make a powerful statement about the heart. Most of us focus and judge each other by external measures. This is not to our benefit. There is great wisdom Paul used in his addresses to the Corinthian and Galatian churches in their unique situations.

The Galatians fell into a horrible trap that was embraced at a heart level. They thought they were doing right by adding law to Jesus. It was not just about having a wrong identity; they were mixing in a little leaven that would destroy the power of grace from working in their lives. Even Paul asked how miracles ever came into the congregation. Was it by hearing of faith, or by their working laws and self-performance righteousness? They knew they experienced the miraculous power of God by hearing and believing, not by doing righteous acts on their own ability. The Galatians were moving into very dangerous ground by believing the law to save them over Jesus. After all, isn't that what spun most of mankind into what we know as the 'Dark Ages'? More accurately speaking, the Dark Ages of the church?

Now, the Corinthian church was not consciously trying to dishonor God. They were just caught up in a fleshly mind-set. They had lots of things to learn about regarding their new position in Christ. Truly their main problem was an identity crisis. No one can live contrary to the way they see themselves within their own heart. These Corinthians were not consciously aware of their new identity or position in God through Jesus. Thus they lived like they thought life should be in order to fulfill whatever desires they had.

IDENTITY

Let me give another quick example. In years past I had witnessed situations where several youth I knew personally had been sexually abused. I remember these kids were so sweet before the incident, but not long afterwards they began to change. I was baffled by the fact that the very thing that hurt them so bad, was what they began to gradually draw toward. It confounded me and my logical reasoning. Why? It took me several years of seeking to learn the answer to this and the knowledge of how to help someone in that scenario. You guessed it: It is the heart.

When these kids were abused, the abuse affected their emotions, thoughts, and feelings, leaving deep scars in their innocent hearts. They did not have the foundation to control the negative outside influence and reclaim their heart from abusive input. It opened doors for the enemy to come in and speak lies to them. Satan began to tell them that they were impure, unloved, tainted, dirty, used, abused, and the like. When you hear those words and embrace the emotion and belief, you write some strong core beliefs in your heart. Before you know it, you are living out what was put into your heart. Your heart is designed to do everything in its power to fulfill what you put in it. It is intended to be a great blessing to you, but you still have the power to choose, or esteem, death over life.

Your heart is designed to do everything in its power to fulfill what you put in it.

At this realization, I understood the answer was to speak *life* into someone who has been badly wounded by another person. The answer is to remind such people how pure they are, to let them know how loved they are, and to tell them that they are more valuable than anything else on earth. I should rebuild their sense of worth and value with God, encourage them in their righteousness, and let them know that they can turn to God and He will hold and take them through the rough times in life. I should tell them that God sees them as holy and perfect without any spot or wrinkle because Jesus Himself had washed them. Their spirits are sealed with the Holy Spirit, and they should focus on their true identity. People will live out life the way they view themselves.

When we lose our identity, we will do all kinds of weird things that don't make any sense. We all have watched people act ludicrous and immaturely for their age. I have watched full-grown men throw temper tantrums that would make a ten-year-old embarrassed. I am appalled to see some of the things people do who do not know truth.

Even Jesus had to establish His heart on His identity, who He was, while on this earth. The Bible points out that Jesus came to earth as a man. He lived like any other human would. He was a baby, He needed His diapers changed and everything else that goes with the development process. There are several verses that mention Jesus' humanity, but one such is Luke 2:52: "And Jesus increased in wisdom and stature, and in favour with God and man" (KJV). Throughout Jesus' entire life you will find that He was challenged as to His identity. Look at His temptation. Satan persistently asked Him that "*if*" He was the Son of God, to do a certain task. One of the main temptations was challenging Jesus' identity. Satan tried to get Him to prove who He was. Isn't that where Adam and Eve messed up? They did not *believe* who God said they were and thought they needed something more, so they ate the forbidden fruit.

Even on the cross Jesus was pressured to demonstrate who He really was. The soldiers and even the thief next to Him challenged His identity and told Him to prove that He was the Christ by coming down off of the cross. In the world's minds they would not believe unless Jesus proved Himself. But, Jesus did not need proof; He believed, and His heart was firmly established in the identity God saw Him as. This is where we too need to follow the example of Jesus.

To conclude with my story of the Corinthian and Galatian churches to the mother of the twenty-one-year-old son, let me say this. We ought to stop judging each other's validity of salvation. Let us understand what is going on in the heart before we make accusations and judgments. Like Paul, let's believe that God will finish the work that He started in the believer. We ought to build up and remind one another of our identity and position in Christ until it is so firm in our hearts that not even death could shake us out of our foundation of the identity of who we are in Him.

We ought to build up and remind one another of our identity and position in Christ.

Let us also follow Paul's example to our fellow brothers and sisters. We ought to be strong against any gospel that rises against our righteousness apart from the finished work of Jesus alone. Regardless what religious leader, pastor, or priest we have; no one is to ever tell us that we have to add one thing to what Jesus accomplished for us in order for us to be right with God. Let us encourage one another about our security in God—that we who believe are the saints, even if someone is making poor choices.

Before we shun people, how about we build them up and remind them of who they truly are? We ought to extend grace toward someone just like our own heavenly Father has with us (Galatians 6:1). The Corinthians were neither rebellious nor legalists. People do not become Christians and then instantly perform perfect lives. Rather, they begin an exciting process of freedom. That freedom could take minutes, days, or years for various areas of life, but nonetheless it is freedom. We as leaders must recognize the process it takes for change to become true transformation. We cannot demand someone to not make any mistakes. Even if one is struggling to come out of a sinful life, it will take the person time to read what is in his or her heart, why it is there, and then remove it and replace wrong beliefs with truth. Howbeit, that is something only the Holy Spirit can reveal to someone. It is simple, but simple does not necessarily mean easy. Those things in a person's life did not get there over night. Just the same, it is not always an overnight process for the Lord to walk with someone out of the carnal lifestyle, although it can be.

I feel the need to emphasize one last note. In the instance of the twenty-one-year-old man, who was struggling to have freedom from a sinful lifestyle, he was very much like the Corinthian church. This being so, I approached the scenario from the same stance as the apostle Paul did when in a similar situation. If this young man was resisting sound advice and loving his worldly lifestyle more than his Lord Jesus, then I would have used another method, similar to how Paul dealt with the man who was sleeping with his stepmother and boasting about it to the other Christians. Paul literally delivered him over to Satan for the destruction of his flesh so that his spirit might be saved (1 Corinthians 5:5). (I'll cover more of this in upcoming chapters.) This was because the man would not heed instruction, but rather chose the death and corruption of the world, purposefully bringing it into the church.

Further, I would have taken yet another approach if the man was bound up in legalism. At that point, I would have been like Paul and the Galatians. He actually told the Galatians that if they thought circumcision was going to somehow make them more holy, then they ought to just cut the whole thing off (Galatians 5:12)! In other words, if someone is going to use the law to try and make him or herself more holy, then I take the approach like the law was meant for: to reveal the truth that no one can keep it and that all have fallen short. Get right down to the heart. If people are legalistic, then give them the law so much until they break and see their need for a savior. If people are childlike in their faith, walking with the Lord, then encourage them to the finish no matter how many blunders they make along the way.

Someone like the twenty-one-year-old man who was struggling to be free from the world, is much more ahead of the game than the glamorous legalistic Pharisee who outwardly has it all together. The twenty-one-year-old man has already hit his knees and knows he cannot please God on his own merit. With him it is merely an identity problem. The legalist, on the other hand, not only has an identity problem, but also still has not figured out his own need of a savior apart from his own "righteous" acts.

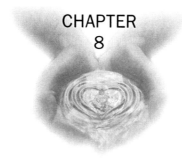

CHAPTER 8

DEAD WORKS

*A*ll too often, I have watched Christians function from the basis of dead works, hoping to reap the benefits that something "dead" cannot bring. It is not that they intended to operate under those ideals; rather, they simply were laboring under a misunderstanding and, more often than not, a combination of misguidance and manipulation from someone they deemed in authority. Dead works are something that external measures alone cannot discern. When we have a solid understanding of the heart, we can begin to recognize how to view our lives in the same way God looks upon mankind. First Samuel 16:7b says, "For the Lord does not see as man sees; for man looks at the outward appearance, but the LORD looks at the heart." So that leaves us to ask, what exactly is a "dead work"? Here are a couple of scriptures to begin with in reference to what the Bible calls a *dead work*.

> *Therefore, leaving the discussion of the elementary principles of Christ, let us go on to perfection, not laying again the foundation of repentance from dead works and of faith toward God.*
>
> Hebrews 6:1

How much more shall the blood of Christ, who through the eternal Spirit offered himself without spot to God, purge your conscience from dead works to serve the living God?

                                        Hebrews 9:14 KJV, emphasis added

Getting the understanding and discernment in our own lives as to whether or not we are living out our salvation by *dead works,* or the inverse of what I will refer to as a "living work," is our responsibility. It is our job to examine our own hearts as to why we do what we do. To better understand ourselves in this area, we must look deeper into what makes a *work* dead. Let's take a look into another passage of scripture to help define this idea of a dead work.

But do you want to know, O foolish man, that faith without works is dead?

                                        James 2:20

Consider this for a moment. The Bible considers faith without works, or actions, to be dead. Another way of saying this is that that kind of faith is lifeless. True Bible faith always has actions to it. The Greek word for "belief" is also synonymous with obedience. What Jesus demonstrated for us is a simple fact that that which you believe, you will act upon. It is much like Daniel says in Daniel 11:32: "…but the people who know their God shall be strong, and carry out great exploits." When people know God—or we could say have a healthy, vibrant faith in their God—they naturally are inspired to do things that without faith they would not find it in themselves to do. When faith is genuine, it always will be attached to works, or action.

Now, let's change this concept around and look into the converse effect. Here is where the idea of *dead works* comes into play. If we have actions, or works, but no faith, then that work we are doing is considered dead. Without faith it is impossible to please God (Hebrews 11:6). Howbeit, there is one more element that we must bring to light in order to properly understand this concept of *dead works.*

First, please understand that we are not studying faith. If we were, I would point out that pure faith is always inspired by love (Galatians 5:6).

Rather, we are focusing here on works, and dead works to be more specific. Since the God-kind of faith is always inspired by love, then we know that the "living works" also should have some element of love involved. Look at what 1 Corinthians 13 says in this regards:

> *Though I speak with the tongues of men and of angels, but have not love,*
> *I have become sounding brass or a clanging cymbal. And though I have*
> *the gift of prophecy, and understand all mysteries and all knowledge, and*
> *though I have all faith, so that I could remove mountains,* ***but have not***
> ***love, I am nothing.***
>
> 1 Corinthians 13:1-2, emphasis added

So, if you are doing all the right actions and have all the outward appearances of holiness, but no faith and most importantly no love, then you can say that your actions are considered dead works. If you do the right thing for the wrong reasons, you will mess yourself up! This is supposed to be an elementary doctrine of your faith and New Covenant position. I trust that the pieces of the puzzle are starting to come together by this time. However, it is still an incomplete thought. Let's look at this concept from a couple more vantage points.

WILLINGNESS

Willingness has everything to do with the heart. Another way to translate the word for "willing" or "willingness" in the Word of God is to substitute it with the word *voluntary*, or "to embrace with the heart." Willingness has everything to do with *dead works*. Willingness is another way for me to clear up the thought of what a dead work versus a living work is. Look at what the Lord said about willingness through the prophet Isaiah:

> *If ye be willing and obedient, ye shall eat the good of the land.*
>
> Isaiah 1:19 KJV

You see, outward actions are not enough. When we give in to false prophets and religion that pressure us to do things solely based upon external or outward works, we have succumbed to *dead works*. Many times people stand behind pulpits and titles trying to manipulate others with their emotions to do things that are contrary to their willingness. By focusing on mere *obedience* apart from *willingness*, we forfeit the good of the land. Or we could say we forfeit the reward and promise from God. Mere obedience (or works) apart from faith, through the basis of love, is nothing more than a religious act. When we do that, we have our reward from men, but neglect the reward from God (Matthew 6:2).

These are powerful statements I am making, but it is long past the time we should start hearing the truth. Far too many believers are burned out from spinning their wheels in the mud of religion trying to please God through the approval from men. It is similar to the story my old pastor used to tell about the boy whose teacher told him to sit down in his chair while in her classroom. The boy finally, out of fear for punishment, sat down, but exclaimed, "I may be sitting down, but on the inside, I'm standing up!" Religious pressure is no way to win someone to Christ. For too long, people have used religion to "clean up and fix people." We have focused on fear tactics and guilt to get people to tithe, attend church programs, look right, and do right. In a nutshell, we have introduced the letter of the law back into the church.

Am I saying that doing right and living right is bad? Certainly not! I'm saying that our methods have not always been godly. Often we have traded the methods of God's wisdom for the wisdom of men. Take, for example, tithes and offerings. Again, realize I am not teaching on tithes and offerings; I am using these to make the point of willingness. Before I continue, though, know this: I am very much for giving to the Lord my finances. It is a way that I can take something temporal and physical and turn it into something spiritual and eternal.

DEAD WORKS VERSUS A WILLING HEART

Before we get into the example of tithes and offerings, let's take a look at someone who disregards willingness and obedience to follow the life of God and engage his or her heart outside of His design. Let's say a person is craving to have an adulterous affair outside of marriage. The person meditates upon what it would be like. He or she dreams about cheating on his or her spouse and loathe the idea of being married to one person. Would that individual have done the deed in his or her heart? Yes. Jesus said that in God's eyes the person already has committed adultery when he or she began to lust in the heart. Now, if the person was able to restrain him or herself from following through in the physical reality, that person will have saved him or herself from great consequences in the natural world. However, he or she will have polluted the heart just as though the adultery had been committed. This person and his or her family still will suffer because of the condition the person chose to allow his or her heart to be in. The spouse will begin to feel the coldness and lack of love; the children will suffer losing the attention and care of the parent. That person in lust will have to purify all that he or she had written on the heart, in order to straighten out the error of his or her way and come back to the purity of love.

People living in an adulterous lifestyle from the heart is operating from a sense of lack. Though externally everything may look like they are perfectly content, there is a storm brewing beneath the surface. Their external good works have turned into works that bear no fruit, for the outward actions do not fall in line with the condition of the heart. In other words, on a spiritual plane their marital faithfulness has become a dead work. People cannot live contrary to the way they see themselves on the inside. So, either adulterous people eventually will act on the internal vision, or they will catch themselves and detest where their thoughts are bringing them and come to repentance.

*People cannot live contrary to the way
they see themselves on the inside.*

Now, let's remove willingness from obedience and look at how obedience alone plays out in other areas. Let's use the example of tithes and offerings. If people give their financial seed with motives of financial gain, or do so trying to earn the respect of others by giving in to the peer pressure of what others might think, then they too have stepped into a dead work that will not profit them internally.

I believe that there is a spiritual principle of giving. If people are able to plug their heart and mind into the heart and mind of God, they will perceive a world of abundance and provision. If people are stingy, their whole world is a world of lack. They are always penny-pinching trying to hold on to everything they get, because in reality they don't believe God is a generous God or that He is their source. Their lifestyle of greed or stinginess reveals their perception of the world: death.

God promised that life and death, positive and negative, are always around us to choose from. Choosing to live a life of giving can happen only if we have a sense of abundance. In order to have this sense of abundance, there has to be a source. The source is an abundantly generous God. When I choose to yield to acknowledge His generosity, I then am preparing my heart to perceive the abundance, life, and positive all around me. My perception will change in order to perceive the life all around God has prepared for me to choose. Having the heart of a giver causes me to perceive the generosity of God. Once I perceive His generosity, I can then believe and receive the promises He has stored up for me through Jesus. This abundant living is a choice. It is not squandering what He gave to me to care for; rather, it is a state of being where I can experience feeling wealthy regardless of external situations. The giver's heart is a doorway that restores the sense of dignity and honor given to us as the kings and priests of God.

Take from among you an offering to the LORD. Whoever is of a willing heart, let him bring it as an offering to the LORD: gold, silver, and bronze.

Exodus 35:5

Before I move into my next point, let me make one side note. A preacher, teacher, or some other leader in your life may be pointing you into the direction of truth. Just like here in Exodus 35:5, Moses was relaying God's heart and feeling about a particular offering. Moses was not using this as a vise to manipulate the people into giving. He simply gave them the opportunity to sow or not, completely free of obligation. "But this I say: He who sows sparingly will also reap sparingly, and he who sows bountifully will also reap bountifully. So let each one give as he purposes in his heart, not grudgingly or of necessity; for God loves a cheerful giver" (2 Corinthians 9:6-7).

You may not have your heart established in God's truth about a given scenario, but it is not for me to criticize and condemn you for your lack of maturity or readiness. I may challenge you to keep hot after God, but never apart from love. All of life is a process; maturity is not something that happens over night. We as ministers of the gospel are to recognize and give people time to come into a place of willingness and growth with God. Jesus never once gave someone a guilt trip or used manipulation to get someone to believe or do some work for Him.

Now, let's move on. Notice here in Exodus 35:5 that God gave a command to take the offering from someone who is of a *willing* heart. If you read further in Exodus chapter 36, you will find that Moses had to tell the people to stop giving because they gave more than was needed. This was because they had gotten their motives right. Your offering is not pleasing to God if you are of a grudging heart. A cheerful heart is what pleases God. Jesus said that the children are not subject to a tax (Matthew 17:25). Servants and subjects pay obligatory tribute; the sons have no need to. Hear what I am saying. Many Christians today give out of an attitude of "servanthood," not yet recognizing that they have been adopted as sons by God. Other Christians use their sonship as a reason not to give—but they miss the mark as well. A true son, though not under the same obligation as the servants, will pay tribute and serve his father more than all of the servants if he loves his father. A son will work long hours after all of the servants have gone home and back to their families.

Consequently, our heart will determine the generosity we perceive our God to have. Thus, our heart determines our own generosity and giving. God looks at our attitudes and the conditions of our motives. Ask yourself sometime, "Why do I tithe or give offerings?" Many times our tithing is a dead work, but our offerings are a living work. We often tend to drudgingly give ten percent. Yet, when it comes to giving to special needs or investing in ministries abroad, we give because of our willingness and inducement by love. It is the difference between the person who loves speeding but obeys the speed limit out of fear of getting caught, and the person who follows the speed limit out of love for those around him. It's same end result (obedience) with two different motives (fear versus love).

Our heart determines our own
generosity and giving.

From a personal note, I myself had noticed this feeling of obligation in the past and decided to do something about it. I changed my perception from looking at tithe as a law, to an opportunity to give out of the gratitude and love in my heart toward God. I still gave out of a firstfruits principle, but I released myself from the sense of a tax code. After doing this for a year, I checked my giving statements and found that I gave well above ten percent. My giving was altogether closer to fifteen to twenty percent. That was a huge amount, especially when knowing the budget Andrea and I were living on.

If you find yourself getting hung up on obligation, you don't necessarily have to stop what you are doing. Instead, take the time to adjust your heart motivation. You are to use this principle in everything you do. Remember the story of the widow, who gave two mites at the temple, whom Jesus said gave more than anyone?

> *So He called His disciples to Himself and said to them, "Assuredly, I say to you that this poor widow has put in more than all those who have given to the treasury; for they all put in out of their abundance, but she out of her poverty put in all that she had, her whole livelihood."*
>
> Mark 12:43-44

Notice Jesus was not focusing on how much people gave. What He was noticing was the heart and worship of the giver. In fact, the only time we see God glorying in people's giving is when they gave from an overflow of gratitude, holding nothing back. It is when they worshipped God in their spirit of giving as well as in the obedience of it. When Jesus spoke about the widow giving more than anyone else, He was not referring to her giving more money than anyone. He was looking at the heart. That woman needed her money more than anyone, yet she gave in spite of her need! Others came and made an open show of giving to earn the respect from other people about their good deeds. Their giving had nothing to do with gratitude and worship toward God. It was about feeling good and getting the approval from the church leaders of the day, and thus the approval and awe of the congregation. Like I said earlier, they received their reward from men at the sacrifice of their reward from God. How? By their works lacking the life-giving mixture of love and faith, consequently leaving their works dead before God.

Lastly, to finish up with this aspect of willingness, I would like to end with the story of Martha and Mary. If you've been in church circles long, you may know this story by the phrase, "Martha, Martha!" Jesus was visiting their home and Martha used her gifts of hospitality to serve Him and the disciples. Mary, on the other hand, decided to not serve, but to do what was in her heart, which was to sit at Jesus' feet.

MARTHA, MARTHA

But Martha was distracted with much serving, and she approached Him and said, "Lord, do You not care that my sister has left me to serve alone? Therefore tell her to help me." And Jesus answered and said to her, "Martha, Martha, you are worried and troubled about many things. But one thing is needed, and Mary has chosen that good part, which will not be taken away from her."

Luke 10:40-42

I have heard many sermons about this story and generally they point out that Mary did the good thing and Martha should have done what Mary was doing. Then the messages tend to go on and ask if we are running around working or if we are sitting at Jesus' feet like Mary did. This is definitely one way to approach the truth in this story, but I'd like to look at another angle. First Corinthians 12:28 actually says God gives gifts of helps. This means that some people have a gift of serving. They are just wired to serve others and it actually gives them a sense of fulfillment. Also, in 1 Timothy and many other places, we are told that all leaders in the church should be given to hospitality. So to say that Martha should have been sitting next to Mary, I believe, is but a half-truth.

When God puts it in someone's heart to serve and show hospitality to you, it is rude of you to not receive. Hospitality is that person's expression of worship to God. That person is at that moment being a living sacrifice, as the Word so eloquently puts it. There was nothing wrong with Martha serving Jesus and the disciples. What was wrong, however, was her attitude. She served out of obligation. She was, in essence, operating in a dead work before God. In order to transition from a dead work to a living work, she only needed to adjust her heart.

If Martha was serving Jesus from a stance of worship and honor to serve, she would have cared less what Mary was doing. And by doing so, she would have received recognition from God, even if man did not notice. After all, the Bible says in Psalm 75 that it is God who gives promotion, not man. So, who cares what men think of us? Are we God pleasers or man pleasers? For Jesus to say Mary did the right thing by sitting with Him was because that was what was in her heart. As far as Jesus was concerned, Martha may as well have sat down too, for she was serving out of an unwilling heart, which in turn is no service to God at all.

I have focused a lot on willingness. Note that there will be many times your heart really does not want to do what is right. Those are the times when you need to take a moment to yourself, whether seconds, minutes, or days, to do the necessary heart work—the kind of heart work that alters your willingness to function out of faith and love as something genuine. Let me give you a quick example of what I am referring to here. Recently, I had several persons in a church leadership position come against our ministry rather harshly, even though they never have taken the time to get to know us. They stirred up accusations that were rather absurd. The truth of the matter was that they only knew how to minister out of the logical mind. They were having a hard time grasping the concept of the heart, and because of their lack of understanding, they stirred up accusations. A few days later I lay in my bed meditating on what the Lord had for me to do for the next few weeks. He spoke so very clear within my heart. He said, "Why are you allowing these people to distract you away from what I have given you to do?" Jesus was absolutely right! These accusations were stealing away my focus and time. The Lord very clearly put it in my vision to finish writing the book you are now reading. The best thing I could have done to resolve that conflict was to get my own heart right, stop pondering what their motives could be, and move on. It is not my job to judge people's motives or hearts. Those brothers in the Lord now hold no more power over my thoughts or focus. I am able to get back to the vision of love and walk forward in faith.

If God has given you a gift, then use it with a willing heart. It is easy to get caught up in the social status frame of mind in today's manmade societies. Be on guard as to what your motives are in serving and giving; examine how you approach everything. Don't be afraid to say, "No." I remember when I first began to volunteer in my church. Some of the best advice my dad gave me was the freedom from obligation. He told me that when people see you as a servant, they can tend to take advantage of it. Before long you feel that you "have" to commit to this and that, and not much later you are burned out. This can get quite unhealthy and lead you into dead works. Be on guard with your heart. Learn to master yourself. You profit nothing when your works and performances are missing the life element of the heart (1 Chronicles 29:9).

SUPPORT

*Then the people rejoiced, for that **they offered willingly, because with perfect heart they offered willingly to the LORD**: and David the king also rejoiced with great joy.*

1 Chronicles 29:9 KJV, emphasis added

Andrea and I decided in the beginning of our ministry to always be on guard against bringing our supporters into dead works. Now, don't read more into this than what I'm saying. Andrea and I believe in sowing good seed. We believe in helping people understand the principles of giving, sowing, and reaping. They are very real spiritual laws and principles. However, they can become very *dead* laws and principles as well.

Those times when we are tricked into giving for the sole purpose of getting something back, we really have no pure motive at all. James 4:3 says, "Ye ask, and receive not, because ye ask amiss, that ye may consume it upon your lusts" (KJV). The word here, *amiss*, translates to sick, evil, or badly in reference to morally.[1] When we do not have purpose beyond ourselves, we are not Kingdom-minded nor are we guided by love. Deuteronomy 8:18 says that God gave us wealth in order to establish His covenant on this earth. We should desire to use prosperity for others and honor God by establishing His Kingdom on this earth by our increase. However, prosperity is not so that we can focus on and feed our greed and lust for material possessions.

Don't misinterpret what I'm saying. I do believe in prosperity and the promises of God that all that my hands find to do will be blessed. But, I am not in favor of seeking God for the sole purpose of personal gain and self-glorification, stroking the ego in some pharisaical attitude.

First Timothy 6:5 says, "Perverse disputings of men of corrupt minds, and destitute of the truth, supposing that gain [translates to 'money-getting'[2]] is godliness: from such withdraw thyself" (KJV). Further, Jesus said that you can't be His disciple unless you die to self. Dying to self is not self-abasement; it is simply not centering the world around you and your personal lusts! Within your heart you are embracing Jesus' life, truths, and philosophy above your own. God promised to bless and care for all of His children. You and I have an amazing inheritance; it is just that we take a humble approach with a servant mentality compelled by love.

Dying to self is not self-abasement; it is simply not centering the world around you and your personal lusts!

With all that being said, Andrea and I made a covenant with ourselves that this is God's ministry. Since God was guiding us, He also would provide for us. We would not need to give into fear and try to manipulate or persuade people that they needed to back or support us. We made the decision to never show pictures of poverty and need to play people's emotions and by so doing reach into their wallets for financial support. The Holy Spirit is leading us, and He will show us what to focus on and what is next each step of the way.

---

1 James Strong, *The Exhaustive Concordance of the Bible* (Nashville, Tennessee: Holman Bible Publishers, n.d.), #G2560

2 Ibid., #G4200.

He speaks to His people, and they hear His voice. We knew that God would use whoever, or whatever, to continue to send us out. Further, we decided that this ministry would not become our identity. If God asked us to lay it down, we have prepared our hearts to obey with gladness. I am a mason by trade and have owned two businesses. Hard work is not something we fear.

GOOD WORKS

For we are His workmanship, created in Christ Jesus for good works, which God prepared beforehand that we should walk in them.

Ephesians 2:10

We were not created to live *for* God in the way most have conceived in their minds. We were created for God to live through us! Most would read Ephesians 2:10 and say, we have to do this and that to keep God happy! Wrong covenant thinking! Once again, God is more concerned about our heart than anything else. "There is a vast difference between being saved *by* good works and being saved *unto* good works. Good works do not gain us salvation but they do affirm that salvation has been received into one's life. Good works cannot produce a new nature but a new nature should produce good works."[3]

God has ordained a perfect plan for each of our lives (Jeremiah 29:11). But God does not force that perfect plan upon us. We have been given choice, and the choice between life and death that is constantly around us in any environment is completely up to us. We are the ones who choose in any circumstance to make that moment a living heaven or living hell (Deuteronomy 30:19).

So what are the good works and what does it mean for God to live through us? Romans chapter 7 is about Paul's acknowledgment that in his own ability through the flesh he cannot live the spiritual life. Many Christians are frustrated because they attempt to live out an impossible lifestyle by their own self-will. Christian living is not just difficult living; it is impossible living. No one can live this life in his or her own ability unless

---

3 Andrew Wommack, *Andrew Wommack Living Commentary* (Bible software program).

empowered by the grace of Christ through the Holy Spirit. And to add on that, no one can move into the grace of Christ unless God first has his or her heart. Once a person's heart is yielded to God, only then can that person effortlessly live the Christian life that would otherwise be impossible based upon self-will.

Just as He chose us in Him before the foundation of the world, that we should be holy and without blame before Him in love, having predestined us to adoption as sons by Jesus Christ to Himself, according to the good pleasure of His will, to the praise of the glory of His grace, by which He has made us accepted in the Beloved.

Ephesians 1:4-6

God has chosen you to be holy and without blame through Jesus because of His love. He predetermined to adopt you into the family through His grace, and now you are accepted in the Beloved because of Jesus, not because of your performance. You cannot earn or qualify yourself to walk in the spirit. God qualified you! So don't try to do good works anymore from a sense of earning something from God, thus creating a *dead work*. Colossians 1:12 says, "Giving thanks to *the Father who has qualified us* to be partakers of the inheritance of the saints in the light" (emphasis added).

Ephesians 4:24 says, "And that you put on the new man which was created according to God, in true righteousness and holiness." When you live life according to what God has done in you, your living will transform effortlessly. You will no longer be a slave to a performance mentality. No one will be able to seduce you into dead works by compulsion or a sense of lack before God. When you know your identity, when you know who you already are in Christ, you will live by the law of liberty. A sense of freedom will permeate your entire soul and free your mind from legalistic control.

For you, brethren, have been called to liberty; only do not use liberty as an opportunity for the flesh, but through love serve one another.

Galatians 5:13

Our freedom and liberty in Christ was not give us so we can go live in debauchery, fulfilling our lusts of the flesh while having God's approval! It is so that we could be set free to live out of our hearts before God! The law kept men's hearts hidden. Grace came with truth through Jesus. Grace reveals the truth of men's hearts. We are free to live from the heart before God. That is what God always desired: a love that was sincere. He did not want posers acting a lifestyle they were not truthful about.

Under the law you had to live an outward life; your acceptance was based on your performance. Under grace you are accepted in the Beloved. Sin has no more dominion over you (Romans 6:14). Therefore, you can freely express your life to God apart from focusing on keeping all kinds of man's ordinances. You can express your gratitude and love toward God freely and in freedom from the sense of obligation. You have been set free!

Genesis 47:25 says, "So they said, 'You have saved our lives; let us find favor in the sight of my lord, and we will be Pharaoh's servants.'" This is an excerpt of what the Egyptians told Joseph after they realized the magnitude of their salvation by the wisdom of Pharaoh heeding Joseph's advice. This is an awesome illustration of what happens to the heart of a believer when that person comprehends the magnitude of the salvation of God through Jesus.

The Egyptians were left with nothing but their lives after the famine was over. However, they came to Pharaoh with heartfelt gratitude and appreciation for their salvation on earth. This is an example of you and me when we grasp the love of the Father for us. When you discover the richness of His love and limitless grace poured out to you, your heart will melt and you will effortlessly live holy without even trying. You will live a life of *good works* that God had already prepared for you to enjoy because it will be the simple expression of your love in reciprocation of His for you.

This is a good or living work, one that comes genuinely from the heart. It is motivated by love. It is the simple faith of believing in and who your heavenly Father is. It is an expression of your gratitude and deep appreciation, of your trust in Him. He is your everything. He is your joy and your reward in life. He is the fountain of life, the source of your existence. *Living from here, from the secret place of the heart, you will never have to question if your works are dead or living.* Simply live and enjoy life like a child again. Shed the excess baggage of a performance mentality; you have been set free to live liberated from the approval of men and focused on the approval from God.

PART II

Entering the Power of the Heart

CHAPTER 9

A PERFECT HEART

With all of this talk about the heart, there is one question that needs asking: "Can we ever hope to attain a perfect heart?" Is there even such a thing as a perfect heart in this physical world? Even considering the thought of saying "yes" sounds frightening, for it seems almost sacrilegious to think we can be perfect of heart. Yet, as we begin to remove the shackles of religion that have devalued us and created fortified walls that impede us from entering the simplicity of the heart realm, we will see a completely different vantage point. For those who have experienced the new birth in Christ, it is our longing and desire to have a perfect heart (1 John 3:3). This desire alone signifies the existence of the perfect heart as a potential reality. After all, it is God who gives us the desires like His in our hearts, and He intends fully to bring those desires into being (Psalm 37:4).

The answer to our question is a definite "Yes!" Yes, we absolutely can hope and expect to have a perfect heart before the Lord if that is the choice we make. Notice, mind you, that I said *before the Lord*. This I will explain in more detail as we move forward.

PREPARATION

Then He said to them, "Take heed what you hear. With the same measure you use, it will be measured to you; and to you who hear, more will be given."

Mark 4:24

Jesus made a statement about the heart of passion and dedication. It is a principle of preparation. This principle basically is saying that you will get out only what you put in. For example, someone who practices martial arts knows better than to get in a training hall mentality. In other words, when in practice, if you only put in the halfhearted effort of thinking, *"This is only practice,"* then you will acquire very little skill. Simply, if you put in little effort, you gain little measure in return. This principle applies to all of life.

In addition to this is the realization of need. There are many things I did not value until later in life merely because I never saw the big picture of their importance. I even can remember my first taste of college. During my high school years, I thought once I attained the status of college student I would have no more worries and life would be mine for the taking. I would be free from parents and rules, living carefree besides maintaining a job or business. After all, that was what was portrayed through movies, television, and the unknown ahead. They confirmed that must be what life was about. Wow, what a reality check when I realized life was not what I imagined! It wasn't long before I missed having a home to go to, food in the fridge, and free laundry, and rules did not seem that bad anymore. At that point I changed my perspective and had gratitude where before I had very little. This has everything to do with preparation. I had to experience some hard things before I could see a clearer perspective. These all were preparation for me to embrace and fully appreciate the deeper truths God was trying to speak to me.

So, first we must look at *how* to prepare one's self before we can understand the good fruit of a perfect heart. Preparation is always just as important, if not more, than any actual event. We in our fast-paced culture have very little regard for preparation. This is not to our benefit! We tend to have an event mentality. Generally speaking, our generation attempts to live from one thrill to the next. The mindless masses of man's society seek one event after another without taking time to digest and internalize the lessons learned in the heart. We tend to seek out all the glitz and glory of one meeting, then move on to the next big thing. In essence, we think that these meetings, religious ceremonies, or concerts are going to bring fulfillment, circumventing our own responsibility of participation, as if someone else has the ability to make us whole. That is the way of our microwave ideals we have come to learn in our victim-based culture. In reality, we look everywhere externally for what can come only from within.

The world tries to coach us into believing that we are victims and have entitlement to some pie in the sky. We deserve to be given the goods of everyone else's labors. Why should we have to work hard and learn the values of life, when they are indebted to us? "The government owes me 'such and such,' I deserve 'this and that,' and you make too much money and are obligated to share your wealth with me." These types of statements are a reflection of why people so rarely discover the true ecstasy of truth—they don't believe in the work needed to prepare for it. Yes, I am saying it is priority that we prepare ourselves to receive truth. If there is no preparation, there is very little value for the lessons learned or the wisdom given. Why do we think we can appreciate and esteem an event, a gift, or wisdom with no sacrifice? The greater the sacrifice, the greater the value. Just take a look at the prodigal son. Whom do you think understood the greater depths of the father's unconditional love, the son who stayed or the son who left and was later restored by the father? It did not have to be that way, but if we refuse sound wisdom and personal heart preparation, then we are in store for the school of hard knocks for the preparation.

...and **receive with meekness** *the engrafted word, which is able to save your souls.*

James 1:21 KJV, emphasis added

And he [Rehoboam] *did evil, because* **he prepared not** *his heart to seek the LORD.*

2 Chronicles 12:14 KJV, emphasis added

Here are two examples about preparation. James 1:21 tells us to "receive with meekness the engrafted word." This is telling us what condition our heart should be in, in order to receive the Word of God. Meekness does not just happen robotically. Meekness is an attitude of humility and teach-ability. When people have a meek spirit, they are simply those who do not think of themselves, their opinions, or their denomination more than they ought. Rather, they realize that there is much to learn and that they by no means have all the answers. Meekness is a part of people who are constantly learning, growing, and increasing in wisdom. Meekness does not signify those who are timid. People who are meek generally are people who are confident, and when they speak, they speak with authority. Meekness is the opposite of arrogance. Don't confuse confidence with arrogance. Confidence is assurance of something greater than self, whereas arrogance is self-glorification and pride.

We must prepare by making the decision to read with open heart and humility when we read the Word of God. Instead of interpreting a scripture by what mama taught or what pastor says, we ought to be open to what God is saying when listening and reading the Bible. We ought to challenge ourselves and say within that we do not know every interpretation about words or concepts. Before we read the Word of God, we should have an open heart to learn things we have never been taught. We even should be willing to lay down old beliefs, or doctrines, that may not line up with what the Holy Spirit is revealing through His Word. That is true meekness. If we read the Bible from a "know-it-all" attitude, then we will receive little to nothing in return. Let's be teachable; let us be willing to look at a truth from all different angles and perspectives.

Preparation is a doorway. The doorway is an amazing opportunity to perceive like you never had seen before. Preparation creates the capacity for deep value. Without proper preparation, one can never wholly grasp the deep worth of the thing, truth, or lesson learned. When someone lives a life void of truth, yet knowing there is more, seeking to learn and thrive in life, that someone will glean and cherish the smallest amounts of revelation and insight that he or she had been deprived of for so long. The reason people are frequently neither satisfied nor passionate about the small and simple things of God is primarily because they have never prepared themselves for the rapture in the small or intangible. Most are consumed in a vacuum of the physical world and only see according to the five senses. Truthfully speaking, one can never completely appreciate the grand things of life until he or she has learned to appreciate and discover the beauty in the small. God may speak or give insight that is very simple or short, but people commonly blow it off because it was not as impressive or earth-shaking in comparison with another's testimony. Never allow others to diminish what God gives you. Cherish the little things in life, and allow yourself to feel the rapture in simplicity.

*Preparation creates the capacity
for deep value.*

Having completed the outline of preparation, we can now begin to understand a perfect heart. The psalmist understood this concept all too well. Also keep in mind that it was David, the psalmist, whom the Bible declared to have had a perfect heart. Read here what he said in preparation to a perfect heart:

> *I will sing of mercy and justice; to You, O LORD, I will sing praises. I will behave wisely in a perfect way. Oh, when will You come to me? I will walk within my house with a perfect heart.*
>
> Psalm 101:1-2

> *For it came to pass, when Solomon was old, that his wives turned away his heart after other gods: and his heart was not perfect with the LORD his God, as was the heart of David his father.*
>
> 1 Kings 11:4 KJV

What an incredible statement! First, in Psalm 101, we must notice that David was living a life of seeking the Lord wholeheartedly. He was not out looking for excuses to live his own selfish desires. He was glorifying and esteeming God. From that condition of heart, he was able to declare and make a vow to himself that he would walk even within his house with a perfect heart! This is radical! First, David said he would behave wisely in a perfect way. He was not out trying to use God and get God's blessing to be a fool in life. He was looking and waiting on the Lord to come and visit Him.

From that attitude, he said that even in the privacy of his home, when no one was watching, he would walk with a perfect heart. There were no ulterior motives. It was simple, pure, and genuine.

You may be asking yourself about David's mistakes and screwups that, according to the law, he should have been stoned to death over. It is true that even though the Bible records David as having a perfect heart in God's eyes, he did trip and make a few errors. Although David had an excellent heart, he was not flawless. David did fall short from the standard of the law, but he was perfect in another standard. Ultimately, David sought after God's heart above all else. What is awesome about God is that He is not like physical man! Even though David committed adultery and murder, was a poor father, and brought a curse on Israel that killed many innocent people, God still considered him as having a perfect heart. There are many other scriptures that speak of the perfection of David's heart. In fact, God used David's heart as a standard for future kings (1 Kings 9:4-5).

This sounds absolutely absurd in the natural world's philosophy, especially when you paint a picture of what David's deeds would look like today. Imagine if a leader in your church did all of the things that David did. What would you think about that someone in leadership who made mistakes like David's? Religion teaches us to look at the external and pass judgment. Religion would look no further than the actions and then question that one's very salvation. What would you be tempted to do?

What is even more amazing about David is that after his blunders, God did not remove him from kingship! Oh, how I love the mercy and grace of God! God did not compare David with other people and say his sins were worse than so and so's. However, with King Saul, who made mistakes also, God removed the kingdom of Israel even from his sons. Externally speaking, Saul's sins would have been much more acceptable than David's. Why the difference between David and so many of the other kings who sinned? Why was David still considered perfect of heart after making such errors?

The answer all lies within the heart. When David sinned and his eyes were opened to what he had done, you always can find the Bible recording his immediate, genuine repentance. David never tried to make excuses for his errors. He never tried to claim the victim card and shrug off responsibility.

David never blamed people for what his choices were. He knew no one was ultimately responsible for his own decisions but him alone. David hurt with great pain over his sins, but he never continued in shame over them. After he dealt with the issue, he would pick himself up, let go of any condemnation, and move forward in his call.

Proverbs 24:16 says, "For a righteous man may fall seven times and rise again, but the wicked shall fall by calamity." Being righteous does not mean you never make a mistake. A righteous person may lose priority or let his or her guard down for a moment and make a careless mistake, but because of his or her heart, that person will rise above the calamity. A heart established in righteousness will empower a person to live in victory, let go of shame, and stand back up triumphing over sin in the identity of righteousness. However, a heart not established in righteousness will succumb to the shame and deceitful self-centered lifestyle of sin. That person will see him or herself as sinful and dirty, and because his or her identity is branded on the heart by his or her actions, the person will never rise above the deceit of condemnation.

Take a look at the baby David conceived with Bathsheba. David was broken and humiliated over the evil he had done. He fasted and prayed that God would spare the newborn baby's life and not punish the innocent for his sins. The child ended up dying. David accepted the consequences, knew God still loved him, let go of shame, cleansed himself, and prepared to move forward in newness of a corrected heart. David's confidence in the Lord's love was no excuse to sin; rather, it was an establishment for him to succeed in all of life, not needing sin. Walking in righteousness is not to earn God's love or acceptance; it is simply an establishment of our position here in earth. Jesus established our position with God; we establish our position in earth by the choices we make to walk in or out of righteousness.

Now, take King Saul. Saul always tried to explain his sins and pawn off the responsibility. Saul's heart was not sensitive; nor was it pure in motive toward the Lord. In the final analysis, Saul did not guard or prepare his heart to continue after the Lord. Saul's heart was tainted with selfish ambition; so, little by little he allowed the influence of others in and hardened his heart toward God. It was this hardness of heart that was Saul's demise.

David had prepared his heart. He was soft, pliable, and teachable, and in the end he always esteemed God just for the sake of God. He was not esteeming God to get things. He had a love and special place in his heart that he guarded as the secret place between him and God (Psalm 91).

I trust you are starting to perceive where this is going. You too can have a perfect heart in the eyes of almighty God! It is attainable. It is simple. Simple does not necessarily mean easy. The hardest part of this simple process is taking the time and being honest with one's self. Some will have much pride, selfish ambitions, and shame to let go of before entering the state of perfection. Again, I am not talking about a perfection of flawless moral conduct. I am talking more about a state of being. Obtaining a perfect heart is a state of being, and like any state of being, it is our choice to live with a conscious awareness of that state.

HOW TO START THE PROCESS OF PERFECTION

In Exodus 19 we see an example of the Lord commanding the people to prepare and sanctify (set apart) themselves for the visitation of His presence. All processes start with choice and expectancy. When we go through a transformation, we first make a choice to consider the possibilities. Then, once we see the pleasure that comes with the potential possibilities, we put our hope in the expectation of good. It is then that we make the choice to live or be what God says we "be." But, what is really exciting about the Kingdom of God is that it is entered through our change of thought and belief. "Repent, for the kingdom of heaven is at hand" (Matthew 3:2). *Repent* simply means to change our mind or change our perspective. Once we change our perspective to line up with God's, we can begin to experience the Kingdom of God!

You first must prepare your heart attitude by making a decision. Like David, begin by declaring the same as he in Psalm 101:1. Meditate on God, His kindness, love, and goodness toward you. Feel His affection toward you. Start to acknowledge His best and favor to you. Feel Him. Touch that secret place within your heart that is just meant for you and Him. He has always cared for you. His description is not even closely justified with words. It is not about what He necessarily does for you; it is more simply about who He is! He is everything. He is the source. He is the "I am." You can see David's example of this heart preparation throughout the Psalms.

Now that you are beginning to build your esteem, value, praise, remembrance, and so much else for the Lord, you are beginning to prepare. *Do not try to be, do, or become something; simply open up, yield to, and become immersed as one with the very presence of God. Just be!* Like the "I Am" concept Jesus presented, just be who you are in Him and allow Him to be who He is in you. Allow Him to permeate your very soul. Let every fiber of your being smell of the sweetness and love of God. At this moment, allow a shift to take place and feel the deep and prevailing worth He has for you. Choosing to enter His reality is the preparation. The preparation begins with choice.

Choosing to enter His reality is the preparation.

This is the approach we take to begin the perfection of our heart. The only true reality that exists is the reality of Spirit. And the only true spiritual realities are those of the truth and Word of God. The physical world is a manifestation from the unseen and eternal realm. The unseen is much more grand and powerful than the physical ever could dream of being. The unseen and invisible is the parent force to the tangible and physical. Many of us are uncomfortable with putting so much emphasis on the unseen realities. It is foreign territory, and generally the unknown is feared. The fear of the unknown holds the masses captive from the liberty waiting for them, of living from the realm of the heart.

To have a perfect heart, we begin with choice. Moving on, we begin to act on that choice and esteem God's views and truths as supreme. We ultimately esteem Him above everything in life. Then from there, after making the decision to yield, we embrace the decision. Making an inner vow is exactly what we are doing. Inner vows often are looked on as bad when, in fact; they are just one spiritual principle of writing on the tablet of our heart. Often, we as children make inner vows to our detriment. When we are hurt or abused by someone, we say with deep conviction within our core that we will never do "such and such" or that we will always do "this or that." Thus we create a state of existence that holds our perception in bondage to those limits we have placed within our heart. We are, however, in this case making a vow of freedom: a vow to always perceive, acknowledge, and become aware of Christ in us, the hope of glory, no matter what external situation we find ourselves in. This decision to make a vow within ourselves like David's example is but the beginning. We are making a very healthy and godly decision to find fulfillment in our Lord always and esteem Him over everything. After I had a near-death experience with a brown recluse spider, I made an inner vow. In the midst of my passion and inspiration after the healing, I vowed that I always would believe God even until my last breath was gone.

Your motive also must be pure. You are not seeking a perfect heart for any other reason than to truly know your Father for who He truly is and to discover the rapture of life in knowing Him. It is not something to boast about to others; actually, doing so you would reveal your imperfection of heart. It is, rather, a state of being you live from. You will come into a place of confidence. You will begin to discover that you are no longer sin-conscious. Instead you will find yourself being conscious of your righteousness established in Jesus and because of Jesus. It is extremely liberating to live life purely from knowing God. Your fear and torment of coming judgment will melt away. You will begin to intuitively know and understand what the Scriptures meant when they said perfect love casts out fear. You always will know your acceptance and worth with God. These are the marks of a properly established and perfect heart.

I did say you would no longer be sin-conscious. It was God's original design in the Garden of Eden that man not have a consciousness of sin. It was, in simplicity, a life of knowing and walking with God. There was no need to be drawn outside of God for fulfillment. When you are fulfilled in the life of God, you will not know a consciousness of sin. And yet, if you were to veer from the straight path of God, once you recognized it, you would detest it, throw it far from you, and return to righteousness, for that sin is no longer who you are. Sin is not the issue. Your heart is. Jesus dealt with all of the world's sin on the cross. It is now a matter of choosing and accepting Him. What will you choose for fulfillment?

*And thou, Solomon my son, know thou the God of thy father, and **serve him with a perfect heart and with a willing mind**: for the LORD searcheth all hearts, and understandeth all the imaginations of the thoughts....*

1 Chronicles 28:9 KJV, emphasis added

*I beseech thee, O LORD, remember now how **I have walked before thee in truth and with a perfect heart**, and have done that which is good in thy sight....*

2 Kings 20:3 KJV, emphasis added

*Then the people rejoiced, for that **they offered willingly, because with perfect heart they offered willingly to the LORD**: and David the king also rejoiced with great joy.*

1 Chronicles 29:9 KJV, emphasis added

*But the high places were not taken away out of Israel: **nevertheless the heart of Asa was perfect all his days**.*

2 Chronicles 15:17 KJV, emphasis added

I wanted to give a few more examples of those recorded in the Bible as having a perfect heart. You will see that the perfection of heart in God's view is not focused on outward performances. He looks directly at the inward part of man—the heart. He sees your willingness. He sees your attitude and motives. It was never about whether someone "sinned" or not. It always was about walking with a truthful heart without hidden agendas. This is something precious that is only between you and God. No man ever can know your heart. Yes, the fruit of your life will reflect the heart; that is what men can see and examine. However, only God is capable of seeing and examining the heart. This will be your own personal journey and relationship with Him.

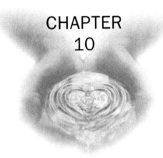

CHAPTER 10

AN UNRIGHTEOUS HEART, YET A RIGHTEOUS SPIRIT?

ow is it possible for a born-again person to live a lifestyle of sin? To what degree does someone have to sin before he or she loses his or her salvation? These are very good questions, and once again they all have to do with a person's heart. In order for me to bring a clear picture to the understanding of the heart, these are questions that I cannot avoid answering.

I say this to your shame. Is it so, that there is not a wise man among you, not even one, who will be able to judge between his brethren? But brother goes to law against brother, and that before unbelievers! Now therefore, it is already an utter failure for you that you go to law against one another. Why do you not rather accept wrong? Why do you not rather let yourselves be cheated? No, you yourselves do wrong and cheat, and you do these things to your brethren! Do you not know that the unrighteous will not inherit the kingdom of God? Do not be deceived. Neither fornicators, nor idolaters, nor adulterers, nor homosexuals, nor sodomites, nor thieves, nor covetous, nor drunkards, nor revilers, nor extortioners will inherit the kingdom of God. And such were some of you. But you were washed, but you were sanctified, but you were justified in the name of the Lord Jesus and by the Spirit of our God. All things are lawful for me, but all things are not helpful. All things are lawful for me, but I will not be brought under the power of any.

1 Corinthians 6:5-12

This has been quite a controversial subject for many believers. It has been said that if you were committing the act of one of these sins and died in that act before repenting, you surely would go straight to hell. It has been used to reintroduce the law back into the church, much like the Galatians did with the event of circumcision. So, the question remains, how do you appropriate this scripture, the heart of a believer, and a perfect new created spirit, holy and blameless in the eyes of God?

This subject came head on years ago when I was talking with an old classmate from school whom I will call Diane. (Diane and her husband are now serving the Lord as missionaries.) We had a chance to meet up at a mutual friend's home. She was sharing her testimony and how much she had changed since her college years. She explained how after her high school years she got sidetracked and slid back into the world. Diane went on to tell me that if she were to have died in that state, she would have gone straight to hell. It was this statement that revealed such a lack of understanding in our contemporary church culture, which I will address.

The heart is deceitful above all things, and desperately wicked; who can know it?

Jeremiah 17:9

Let me begin with this passage of scripture. The translators did a rather lousy job in translating the message. If you'll study it out, you'll find that in the original language of Hebrew, it reads something more like this: "The heart that is incurable, or reprobate, who can know?" Then the next verse goes on to say that only the Lord God knows men's hearts and when they have gone reprobate, or beyond help.

The heart of man in and of itself is not deceitful. Your heart is not trying to lie to you. You may try to hide your heart from others, but when you are quiet with yourself and soul search, the reality of who you are on the inside comes to light. The deception within yourself is when you try to cover up and mask what is taking place within your own heart.

Understand that I am in no way attempting to profess to know man's heart condition. There are, however, some very telltale signs and principles that allow us to read what is in someone's heart. I could never make the statements I am about to make, except for the simple fact that I knew this woman before and after her stint of adapting the world's philosophy as her own.

When Diane told me about her lifestyle of living like the devil, in whoredom, carousing, and a drunken state of mind, I felt nothing but great joy at the reality she had found freedom in Jesus through it all. And once she made the statement of knowing that she had lost her salvation during that period of time, I quickly spoke against that confusion of spirit and heart. To her bewilderment, I laid out the truth that had she died in the midst of her ungodly lifestyle, she still would have gone straight to heaven! She was jaw-dropped, to say the least. Her quick response was that her fruit was that of the devil; therefore, she was exactly a product of what was being produced in her life.

I then affirmed to her that I could not know to make these statements, except for the fact I know her now, and I knew her before. I told her that in the middle of her perverted lifestyle she still thought of God. She always had an inward yearning for His reality even though she did not know how to find it. Without hesitation, she acknowledged that it was true, and she even would preach Jesus when she was drunk out of her mind in the bar. There was always a feeling of desire for her first love. The desire was for the One who first loved her from the beginning: Jesus.

DIFFERENCE OF HEART AND SPIRIT

From here I explained the difference of heart and spirit. I told her the only problem she had was a heart problem, not a spirit problem. No doubt she was living in very dangerous territory, which had the potential to cause her to harden her heart to a point of blatant, flat-out rejection and denial of Jesus Christ, choosing to utterly throw away her heavenly salvation and embrace her sin to such a degree. Sin can lead us so far away from God that in the beginning we forfeit our earthly inheritance of the Kingdom, but it has the power to eventually lead us far enough beyond to reject and ultimately sacrifice our heavenly position too (Hebrews 12:16). It always begins with the heart.

Diane simply had a heart issue. Somewhere along the line she began to have a sense of lack. From this emotional lack with the Lord, she sought to fill it elsewhere. She began to look for it outside of God. This woman let down her guard and was influenced by her so-called friends. She thought that the lifestyle of partying would bring fulfillment, love, acceptance, recognition, and worth. She merely was deceived.

When the apostle Paul said idolaters, adulterers, thieves, gluttons, and so on would not inherit the Kingdom of God, he was talking about living it here on earth. All of these lifestyles Paul listed reveal a matter deeper than outward actions, as most would preach. They reveal the heart. The reason people would walk under the subjection and dominion of these sins is because in their hearts they think those things will bring them fulfillment. They are doing to the best of their ability with what resources they believe are available to them. They believe for fulfillment outside of the Kingdom of God. You cannot believe and operate in the world's philosophy and expect to have the Kingdom fruit of divine peace, everlasting joy, and limitless love to abound.

Once people embrace a deception and believes it is needed for wholeness in their life, they are yielding to that "thing" as their savior in *that* area of their life. As for going to heaven, they may believe on Jesus for their sacrifice, but they may not have faith that Jesus is enough for a particular circumstance or need. How does this happen? Plainly, after their heart was renewed in the new birth, they did not renew their mind, or thoughts. They go back to thinking along their old mentality, thus reprogramming, or writing, on the new heart an old standard. Jesus may be their savior as far as their peace with God is concerned, but they may not make Him Lord over *every* area of their life.

Allow me to put it this way. You can have a perfect and righteous spirit and yet have unrighteous areas of the heart! I will take the rest of this chapter to explain this concept. The woman in the story is a classic example of someone having a righteous spirit and an unrighteous heart. The honest reality is that you don't get saved, lose your salvation, repent, and then get saved again over and over as some would like to think. Your salvation is much more secured in God's hands than that. Yes, you can choose to throw away such great a salvation, but that is not an easy thing to do. And once you do that, you will never have a desire to ever return or seek God again. Your heart would be so cold and rock-hard that you would never want to consider going to heaven with God. To lose the complete salvation of a righteous, regenerated, perfect, and a holy spirit man on the inside can happen only once. Hebrews 6:4-6 says, "For it is impossible for those who were once enlightened, and have tasted the heavenly gift, and have become partakers of the Holy Spirit, and have tasted the good word of God and the powers of the age to come, if they fall away, to renew them again to repentance, since they crucify again for themselves the Son of God, and put Him to an open shame." Personally, I think I only know one person who did exactly that. But, I am not the judge of men's hearts; God is, so I dare not say who is or isn't going to heaven.

JESUS IS NOT ALWAYS IN YOUR HEART…

Jesus promised that He would never leave us or forsake us. As He is, so are we in this world (1 John 4:17). We are His righteousness (2 Corinthians 5:21). Our spirit has been redeemed, and we now wait for the redemption of our bodies and souls. We are holy (Ephesians 4:24). Jesus is in us and we are in Him. What I am getting at is that the Spirit of God is always in our spirit (1 John 4:13). We have the presence of God in us at all times. The fruit of the spirit is always in the spirit. It is our choice whether or not we yield to that fruit for it to operate in our physical lives. By faith we have been made righteous and have a redeemed spirit sealed with the Holy Spirit. Jesus is always within our spirit man.

His presence is always with us. As a brief story, I remember one time I asked the Holy Spirit to remove His gift of speaking in tongues for two minutes so I could again clearly remember what it was like to not have His gift working in me. I was playing with the Lord and was reminiscing what it was like before I was saved. I wanted to have a fresh perspective again of not having the baptism of the Holy Spirit. After asking I thought for sure He would grant me the request. I waited but realized in about five minutes that the Lord would not remove the gift. I asked Him why not, and His response was this: "Son, if I were to remove My ability from you like that, you would never have absolute confidence that I will always be with you." Since God has bound Himself by His Word, He cannot violate or contradict His own Word (Psalm 138:2). Had the Holy Spirit removed His gift of tongues, He would have violated the promise from Romans 11:29, which promises to never remove the gifts and callings. I did not think of that until much later after the Holy Spirit had spoken to me. God is so amazingly good to us!

The Holy Spirit always will be with us. He now lives within our spirit because our spirit has been made righteous. He does not have to come upon us and then leave like in the Old Testament days. The covenant of death and condemnation is now obsolete. We are living in the New Covenant of righteousness (2 Corinthians 3)! If the same spirit that raised Christ from the dead is now in us, and we are righteous, then how come there are times we lack the abundance of life in our souls and physical bodies?

The heart is impressionable. It can be purified, clean, righteous, and then polluted and unrighteous, only to become clean, righteous, and purified all over again. Let's look at some scriptures where we get the idea of Jesus living in our hearts. There are two verses that the church uses for this concept.

That Christ may dwell in your hearts through faith; that you, being rooted and grounded in love.

Ephesians 3:17

Behold, I stand at the door and knock. If anyone hears My voice and opens the door, I will come in to him and dine with him, and he with Me.

Revelation 3:20

Before diving into these verses, we need to comprehend our makeup and where the Lord dwells. We are a spirit, soul, and body. We are a temple of the Holy Spirit. Our spirit has been made righteous. The body and soul are waiting to be fully redeemed, which Jesus will do when He returns. It is in our righteous spirit that the Holy Spirit dwells (Proverbs 20:27). The heart, however, is something that we have complete control over; we determine whether or not the Lord will be present in our heart—and to what degree.

We determine whether or not the Lord will be present in our heart—and to what degree.

Paul had written to Christians when he said, "That Christ may dwell in your hearts through faith…" (Ephesians 3:17). This means Christ may have access to your heart only as you operate in faith. The grace of the Lord Jesus can function through your heart only when you believe! How does this believing happen? Through love! Paul went on to say that the fullness of God can be understood only by being rooted and grounded in the width, depth, and breadth of Jesus' love. From this fullness of love, you can rest in Him and effortlessly yield to His ability working through you.

Next, looking at Revelation, John also was writing to Christians. He said Jesus was standing at the door of the Laodiceans' hearts knocking! In actuality, Jesus was knocking on Christians' hearts, asking them to let Him in! What a powerful report. In context, Jesus said that the church of Laodicea was wealthy, and because of their wealth they thought there was no need for Jesus in their physical lives. These Laodiceans were trusting in their money as their physical source, yet they believed on Jesus for spiritual admittance into heaven. They were rejecting Jesus from entering their hearts, which would have had a ripple effect through their entire composition of spirit, soul, and body. This sounds much like the church of America. We as a nation have greatly resisted the Lord's entering our heart, but we have wanted the "fire insurance" for the afterlife. We have had our physical source of safety, security, and comforts from our own ability and stockpiles of wealth. Many had very little need for Jesus outside of a feel-good Sunday service.

Recently, times have changed. I believe the economic crisis will make many people better for it. Christians everywhere are starting to wake up from the delusion of religion and self-reliance and again are seeking the heart of the Father. You see, you are the gatekeeper of your own heart. You are the one to decide what you will allow access into your heart. Thus you decide the course of your own destiny. Will you choose to rest in His love for you? Will you yield to Him and allow Him access to your heart, letting Him permeate your entire being?

BELIEFS

Proverbs and Psalms speak quite a bit about a crooked, or unrighteous, heart. When a Christian gets born again, he or she is given a new heart. This heart is perfect and soft toward God. Can you remember how, when you first believed, it was so easy and effortless to walk straight in the paths of God? What happened? For one thing, believers often try to understand the power of God through the logical mind. When you do this, you assume that there are things you need to do in your ability to please God; after all, nothing in this world is truly free. At church you may have been told what you had to do to keep God happy, which would enforce the carnal logic. Thus, your heart was polluted to believe God loved you just enough to save you, but you better not mess up, or else…! You were immersed into an Old Covenant mentality of law and condemnation.

Second, and most importantly, you had not renewed the mind to harmonize with your new creation in the spirit. When you faced an adverse situation, or temptation, with time you yielded to some of your old strongholds of past philosophies from the world. As you thought and reasoned with lack of knowledge of God's Word and promises, you may have established your new heart by writing on it old beliefs. This is where purifying your heart comes in. It is one example of what Jesus talked about when putting new wine in old wineskins.

We all have areas in our lives that we are growing in. A perfect heart does not mean a heart that never makes a mistake. It is rather a heart that is seeking and yielding to the truth of God. The Lord is always gently and patiently leading us into His light. He is tremendously kind and affectionate as He walks us out of faulty beliefs or forwardness of heart.

A righteous person, in God's view, is not the same as a righteous person in man's view. Remember, it is the righteousness through right believing alone that is the stumbling stone of the gospel to many. Righteousness is not a matter of moral conduct or moral behavior. Righteousness in God's eyes is lining your heart and faith up with the truth of God. To obtain righteousness for a pure and perfect position in Christ, you simply believe on Christ for righteousness.

> *To obtain righteousness for a pure and perfect position in Christ, you simply believe on Christ for righteousness.*

In the situation of prosperity, you may be currently experiencing physical financial need. But, by your choice to look at the good report, trust God, believe that you are abundantly blessed, and focus on the blessings of the Lord, you are appropriating righteousness. I personally have been in tremendous financial need at times. But, I have never felt poor. I can honestly tell you that I always have felt as though money is a non-issue, even though my circumstances would indicate otherwise. Why is that? Because I have continued to focus on the favor, the opportunities, and potential I have in the ability of God's grace working through me. That is appropriating righteousness in the area of prosperity. It works the same for health. You may be sick and feeling miserable. But, will you choose death, or will you choose to see the end from the beginning? You can operate in fear and expect the worst, or you can hold on to hope and expect the best by holding onto and believing deep in your core the truth of the power of God at work. You decide whether to believe in the power of God or the wisdom of men.

When people have a froward, or crooked, heart, it can mean one of two things. Either their heart is beyond repair and they are reprobate; or, they simply have a false belief in a particular area in their heart. *Froward* plainly means crooked, unrighteous, perverted, or distorted.[1] You can then say that if someone has an unrighteous heart, he or she has a crooked heart. In other words, the heart is not straight, or in line with God's view and opinions.

Think of it like this. The heart is similar to a racetrack. If I have an unrighteous or crooked heart belief in some area of my life, it is bent. Thus, it

---

1 See James Strong, *The Exhaustive Concordance of the Bible* (Nashville, Tennessee: Holman Bible Publishers, n.d.), #G4646.

is not in harmony with God. A straight or righteous heart, however, is right in line with God on His track in perfect harmony with Him and His course. There are many different facets of our lives that we live. All of those areas—from relationships, work, gifts of the spirit, ethics, perspectives, opinions, to daily disciplines and so on—all have to do with areas of our heart. You may have a righteous heart in one area that is in perfect sync with God's Word, but have another area that is crooked as the day is long. There are areas of our lives that may be producing good Godly fruit of life, yet others producing chaos, bitterness, and death. This is all due to the root of the heart in those particular areas.

As I mentioned before, we all have unrighteousness in our heart to some degree in some area that we are working on with the Lord. It is not an excuse to live in stupidity; rather, it is a comfort to know even though the Lord realizes we are not perfect on our own merit, He still wants to work with us to see us come into wholeness. For example, look at the Laodicean model I used earlier from Revelation. The Laodiceans were born again with righteousness, perfection, and sanctification, but they were perverted in their hearts regarding everyday living with the Lord as their source of life. They neglected esteeming Him and keeping their attention on Him in the daily course of life in their abundance.

Daily in our lives the Lord reveals truth to us. The Comforter is always with us, teaching us and bringing us into alignment with Him. As disciples, we are constantly growing and experiencing more and more freedom into the supernatural life of the Kingdom.

DESTRUCTION OF THE FLESH

I opened this chapter with a passage of scripture from 1 Corinthians 6. It is also there that I wish to bring these thoughts to an end. If people are caught up in a sin, it does not signify that they're not going to heaven when they die! Let me take you to an illustration of a real-life scenario Paul had to deal with in the church.

There was a man in the church of Corinth who was so perverted that he was bragging about sleeping with his stepmother. When Paul caught wind of this, he immediately told the church to deliver this guy to Satan. He said that this type of thing was so grotesque that the world rarely heard of such things and "to deliver such an one unto Satan for the destruction of the flesh, that the spirit may be saved in the day of the Lord Jesus" (1 Corinthians 5:5 KJV). Here is an example of an adulterer, fornicator, and someone who under the law would be stoned to death for the incest alone. According to New Testament Scriptures, this man cannot inherit the Kingdom of God. But wait, Paul said to deliver him to Satan so that he potentially could be saved and go to heaven. Case in point is that although he may not have lost his salvation, he cannot inherit the benefits of the Kingdom life of God when yielding to the devil.

You cannot serve two masters. Either you are serving and striving after the desires and purposes of the flesh, or you are serving the purposes beyond self and those of the Spirit. Notice, this man, though living a life of chaos and death, would still have gone to heaven. Paul instructed to deliver him to Satan so that the man might feel the pain and consequences of his decisions and faulty beliefs, to be humbled in hopes that he would come back to the joy of the Lord and not go so far as to throw away his salvation altogether. Later in Paul's second letter to the Corinthians, in chapter 2, he exhorted the Corinthians to forgive and receive back the man whom they earlier had excommunicated.

Did this man lose his salvation and then get it back again? Yes and no. He had lost the physical benefits of salvation given through the promises of God by seeking fulfillment outside of God. But, he never lost his Holy Spirit-sealed righteous spirit. He never lost God's affection, love, and favor. Even though his heart was corrupted, his spirit remained unspotted and pure in the eyes of the God.

Howbeit, once he realigned his heart with the Lord's, he then was open to the mercies and grace of God once again to flow through his life in the physical realities. I am sure there were consequences he would have to live with from mankind for the sins done, however. God may be perfect, but man sure is not. God may know you've changed, but with man it takes a lot of time to build and maintain trust and confidence. Nevertheless, with God all things are possible. He is your shield and great reward.

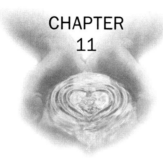

CHAPTER 11

GUARDING AND ESTABLISHING THE HEART

Guard your heart above all else, for it determines the course of your life.
Proverbs 4:23 NLT

*Y*ou and I are commanded to guard our heart above everything and anything in life. Your life is where it is right now because of your heart. Your reality is completely due to the beliefs you have in your heart. Now, you may be questioning the validity of this statement in the scenario of an abusive home, where someone may not be at fault for the hell he or she is living in.

It is very true that we as people cannot always control our external environments or the will of others. There are often bad things in life that happen to us, against our own will. However, we are always in control of our choice. We choose the perspective we will have, whether to see the good or the bad. There is always good and bad, life and death, all around us every moment of every day. The only question is, what will we choose to see? Guarding one's heart is vital to keeping the quality life flow from the spirit alive. Our lives are a product of what we have established in our heart.

For as he thinketh in his heart, so is he....

Proverbs 23:7 KJV

The Hebrew word for "thinketh" is *sha'ar*. This word *sha'ar* translates to estimating as a gatekeeper.[1] This passage from Proverbs then could be translated to say, "As a man estimates in his heart according to the established gatekeepers of his heart, so is he." We hold tremendous power over our own lives through the power of choice. It is our choice whether to believe God in full, or to pick and choose what we will believe based on what we can understand. We ultimately choose our beliefs, and by doing so, we choose our emotions, which then determine our actions and behaviors. Truly, none of us are victims. The victim mentality is an excuse to not lay down our personal views and opinions. One of the outstanding attributes of King David was that no matter what problems he found himself in, he never passed blame. The gatekeepers of our heart that we establish will determine the quality of life we will choose to experience.

A wise man's heart is at his right hand, but a fool's heart at his left.

Ecclesiastes 10:2

This scripture is reiterating the importance of the heart. Here Solomon is saying that a wise person keeps his or her heart in the right hand. In the language Solomon was speaking, he was saying that someone with wisdom will give precedence to the heart as a priority in his or her life. The wise person understands and values his or her own heart above everything. It is a fool who treats his or her heart as secondary. A fool will put other things as priority above the heart, not realizing those things are now in control of his or her heart and ultimately his or her life.

The wise person understands and values his or her own heart above everything.

---

1 James Strong, *The Exhaustive Concordance of the Bible* (Nashville, Tennessee: Holman Bible Publishers, n.d.), #H8176.

Allow me to give a quick example. People who understand how the condition of their heart controls and determines the quality of their life, will more than likely have the wisdom to give priority to their heart. This may be a poor illustration, but it will serve nonetheless. It would be foolish to go out and purchase a new vehicle and then neglect to care for the routine maintenance of the automobile. Everyone knows if he or she wants to have a vehicle that has longevity and good performance, one needs to take care of regular oil changes, tend to the air filter, and so forth. The same is true with the heart. If you want to avoid a frustrated, confused, and emotional rollercoaster ride of a life, then you must have sense enough to daily maintain the control center of your being: the heart.

When you understand the power of your heart, you will begin to pay attention to the subtleties and nuances taking place within you. You will learn to be careful and on guard about what gets sown in your heart. Your heart will be treated with great value, and priority will be given to the health of your heart.

Stand therefore, having girded your waist with truth, **having put on the breastplate of righteousness.**
Ephesians 6:14, emphasis added

How are we to guard and establish our heart? By guarding our heart, we are guarding what we have established regarding what we believe about ourselves and how things work in our lives. Our heart is like an autopilot. The heart is designed to keep our sense of self the same way we believe. Our heart will resist change in the beginning because it is designed to keep us from being affected by outside influences. So then we must ask ourselves what we have believed about ourselves and what we believe about how life works for us. Furthermore, if we lay hold of and continually strengthen a couple simple foundations, those things will prove to be gatekeepers to our heart the rest of our lives, so long as we guard them.

First, though, we must put on the breastplate of righteousness! How? By absolute belief. It is our job to receive the Word of God about our righteousness in Christ. The way we do this is by experiencing the end from the beginning. God gave us meditation as a way to see and experience what our hope is in

Him in order to persuade our heart of that truth and come alive within us.

If you believe on Jesus, then you are as righteous as you can ever be! If you struggle with accepting this, and choose rather to hold on to condemnation and shame, then your life will be ravaged with all sorts of problems, pain, and confusion. So, one of the keys to putting off the negative things that hold you back from believing and to putting on the hidden man of the heart of who we are right now in Christ, is meditation. This is actually one of the greatest persuasions your heart will ever go through: being righteous apart from *your* works, which is the power of the gospel (Romans 1:16).

I will be discussing meditation in the next few chapters, so don't worry too much about what exactly I am talking about. Very simply, it is the ability to see and experience something within our heart. We simply picture with our mind what we intend to see, then begin to feel what that would feel like and experience the joy, peace, and pleasure of experiencing the reality of that truth. We often do this with meditating on the negative possibilities in life. We ought to do this with what God has told us and how His Word will affect us. We may not be able to control all of our external circumstances, but we *can* choose to experience the good and continue in peace through any circumstance. Even when there is great chaos breaking loose around us, we have the choice to be at peace and experience the life of God within us. So, to establish ourselves, we have to feel the emotion and accept what God's truth is toward us and how He sees us.

A quick example would be healing. Believing in healing is not just about believing that it is God's will to heal. Neither is it just about believing whether healing is in the Bible or not. Believing in healing believes that healing is for you and that it affects you. Having information alone will not affect your heart. Your heart is not capable of intellectual information. Your heart stores conceptual information on what your sense of self is and how things relate to you. So, to write on and establish your heart you need more than information; you need to see and feel how that information applies to you. Often we have had wrong opinions on how the Word of God applies or does not apply to us, so we need to correct those misconceptions by allowing ourselves to meditate on how it feels and experience what it is like to have those truths working in us in any environment.

WHAT IS RIGHTEOUSNESS?

What exactly is the concept of righteousness? To make it very simple, righteousness is anything Godly. One of the definitions for the Greek word for "righteous" has a definition of straight.[2] So, you could truly say all the attributes and character of God are righteous (straight). When we believe on Jesus as our righteousness, God then views us by the very righteousness of Jesus. All of Jesus' obedience and perfection becomes ours. When we adopt beliefs and opinions that line up with God's, those beliefs and opinions are then righteous (straight). Just by believing on Jesus as our sacrifice for sins, our spirit became righteous and acceptable to God. However, we may have areas of our personal lives that need to line up with God's ways to harmonize with our new spiritual nature.

WHAT IS THE ARMOR?

Ephesians chapter 6 talks about the armor of God. Do you know what this armor is in reference to? All of the armor is a picture of Jesus! Each piece of armor indicates how Jesus is applied in your life. Second Corinthians 3 says that believers are now under the ministry of righteousness. Even though you may make mistakes, God sees your spirit, the part of you that is holy and righteous. Your heart may have faulty beliefs, but God is not basing your righteousness on your faulty beliefs. The only belief that concerns your righteousness and acceptance before Him is if you received Jesus' payment for your sins.

Some people have done some very funny things in the past in trying to put on the armor of God. The armor is simply a persuaded belief system. All the different areas of the belief system—areas in which Jesus works in a person's life—are illustrated in different parts of armor. When your heart is established in this "armor," then Satan has nothing left to deceive you with. You, in essence, are impenetrable. The one piece of armor, however, that has some of the most importance is the breastplate, which covers your heart. If

---

2 W.E. Vine, *Vine's Expository Dictionary of Old & New Testament Words* (Nashville, Tennessee: Thomas Nelson Publishers, 1997).

you alienate yourself from Jesus' righteousness freely given to you, you will be opening the vulnerability of your heart. One quick blow there from the deception of the enemy, and you will fall apart like shattered glass.

The armor is simply a persuaded belief system.

In 1 Thessalonians 5:8 Paul mentioned the "breastplate of faith." Why did he use faith in Thessalonians, but righteousness in Ephesians? The answer is that your righteousness is based upon your faith in Jesus. Therefore, you are righteous by faith. Your believing on Jesus qualified you for His righteousness. Do you have faith in Him? If so, then you are righteous. This righteousness by faith is the foundation for guarding your heart.

> *But let us who are of the day be sober, **putting on the breastplate of faith and love, and as a helmet the hope of salvation.***
>   1 Thessalonians 5:8, emphasis added

> *Stand therefore, having your loins girt about with truth, and **having on the breastplate of righteousness.***
>   Ephesians 6:14 KJV, emphasis added

Notice how Paul also referred to the breastplate, which guards the heart, as a breastplate of love. The Bible tells us in Jude 20-21 to build ourselves up on our most holy faith by praying in the spirit and keeping ourselves in the love of God. You see, it is our job to keep ourselves in His love. If we refuse His love, we can never have the faith that we are who He says we are. His love is what gives us the ability and strength to believe and accept the righteousness freely given. It is His love that washes away all condemnation.

ESTABLISHED FILTERS

Now that we are establishing our hearts with righteousness, we will be able to use this righteousness as a filter. Whether consciously or subconsciously, we all create filters through which we determine what we will allow or disallow in our heart. Righteousness is the filter we must have in place. With having a righteousness consciousness, we will quickly learn to reject accusations, shame, and a sense of lack from dominating our lives. There is no lack in righteousness. If there were, then God would be a god of lack. His promises even say that the righteous will not go hungry. Let's anchor ourselves firm in the righteousness He has said we are. Let's not let circumstances, performances, or shame tell us contrary to what our true identity is.

There is one more filter which, like righteousness, covers so many other dynamics. This filter is *grace*. I have spoken so much already about this subject, but here is where the rubber meets the road.

> *...For it is a good thing that the heart be established with grace....*
>
> Hebrews 13:9 KJV

> *The grace of our Lord Jesus Christ be with you all. Amen.*
>
> Revelation 22:21 KJV

> *The grace of our Lord Jesus Christ be with your spirit. Amen.*
>
> Philemon 25 KJV

> *I marvel that ye are so soon removed from him that called you into the grace of Christ unto another gospel.*
>
> Galatians 1:6 KJV

Grace is the power of the gospel. I already have covered this in my first field guide, *How to Release the Power of Faith*. Grace also must be our primary filter, with righteousness, by which our heart is established. These two ought to become so ingrained in our thinking and meditating that we cannot separate them from ourselves. It's similar to the way a martial artist would train. In martial arts training, much of the information would never work in real life unless the skill was ingrained into the student's muscle memory. When we are in a real-life, hand-to-hand combat, we do not have time to think. If we have to think about what to do, then we are dead. Our skills, like those of a martial artist, have to be second nature and able to flow without thought.

This is exactly how the filters of faith-righteousness and grace ought to be established in our heart.

Righteousness by faith and grace should be every Christian's default system. With a little time and effort, it won't take long until you can deftly identify and allow or reject the information bombarding you every minute of every day through the filters of life as I call them. In real life, you don't have time to think about every little detail of every word spoken or situation you find yourself in. The guarding system of your heart has to be in place strong enough to function on a subconscious level without your thinking about it.

I can remember back when I began to catch a revelation of these concepts shortly after hearing a preacher. I could identify when he was preaching New Covenant or Old Covenant. I was able to receive the good and spit out the bad. I was elated at the ability to discern the truth. The eyes of my heart were opened; it was at that point my understanding in the Word began to explode.

THOUGHTS

Earlier I quoted a scripture from 1 Thessalonians 5:8, which exhorted us to wear the hope of our salvation as a helmet. The helmet protects the brain. It has everything to do with our thoughts and imaginations. The doorway to our heart is through thoughts, feelings, and emotions. Thoughts in and of themselves are not powerful; it is when we give attention to and attach feeling to those thoughts that they gain power. If a thought has no feeling or emotion, then it has no power and is soon dismissed. Furthermore, we can't be tempted if we have no sense of lack. It is through the imaginations of lack and thoughts of hopelessness that we are led outside of God for fulfillment and into temptation.

If a thought has no feeling or emotion, then it has no power and is soon dismissed.

The helmet of the hope of salvation is the perfect foundation to guard our thoughts. Zechariah 9:12 says that we are prisoners of hope. You and I who are in Christ cannot but help to have hope. We are bound to hope. We have such an incredible Father who loves us beyond all creation. We are His joy and inheritance (Ephesians 1:17-18). Our salvation is not just life after death! Our salvation is health, prosperity, favor, deliverance, safety, and literally anything that pertains to life and godliness today!

Hope translates to a confident expectation of good. There is always good coming. Our future is always good and glorious. We don't always know what may come, but we do know that no matter what life brings us, we will find the good. It's kind of like making lemonade out of lemons. If a few lemons show up in life, God will turn them into lemonade. How, you ask? That is not for us to figure out! It is our job to believe. Then, as the process begins to work, or even afterwards, we are able to understand and see how God is or has worked things out. Let's face it, life is not fair, but God is good! No matter how bad things may look, I have hope. The hope we have will keep us steady and stable through any adversity; it will enable us to find the peace and joy of God in any environment. God is able to finish what He started in us, and He has full intentions of doing so, if we are willing to walk with Him.

THE APPLICATION

Let's apply these truths in real-life application. I have dozens of examples from those close to me who had all sorts of addictions or habits that were killing them. The freedom from their bondages never had to do with people's criticism or condemnation. Rather, it came from the love, acceptance, forgiveness, and grace they received from the Lord. Everyone has a bit of a unique story, but the principles are all the same.

The first step in freedom from a crooked heart is to admit the error. You can experience freedom only to the degree you are willing to deal with your own issues. It is not just admitting our faults, but admitting them with the affirmation that God is still for us and that His love never changes regardless of our actions. More importantly, we need to confirm His love by allowing ourselves to feel and experience His love. Every time I have seen freedom come in people's life, it was when they knew they were loved despite their faults. They were in an environment that allows the process of change without condemnation and judgment.

Allow me to give an example. I had a friend, Tom, who wanted to quit smoking. He tried for more than two years on his own efforts to kick the addiction nicotine had over him. I never criticized his habit, even though his family really could have used the money. He knew it wasn't God's best, but there also was a process happening that required his heart to be involved before the grace of God could be released throughout his being for the power to overcome.

One day, Tom came to me and said he had quit. This time I knew it was different. He finally quit condemning himself and forgave himself for the bad habit, and it was in the forgiveness that he knew beyond reason that God was there to walk him out of smoking. Tom was more than willing to let go and trust God that he had no more need for cigarettes. He said that, in the beginning, every five to fifteen minutes he would feel shaky and begin to have a nicotine fit. In those moments he would call out to God and say, "Lord, You said You wouldn't allow more temptation than I could handle, and I can't handle much; help!" He then relayed that as he focused on the Lord, he would feel a soothing sensation and the "shakes" would go away. He did that every time a craving would hit, until complete freedom was established about a month later. On his own he could never kick the habit. He had to want it bad enough. No one can force someone to change his or her heart. That has to be something one decides on one's own, and from his or her own desire for change.

Other instances I know of are of some who, as they began to catch a revelation of the power of the grace of God, they applied it in the middle of acting out some unrighteous act. Using the example of smoking, those I am thinking of knew they were secure in their salvation, love, and acceptance with Father God, but they also knew the smoking could lead to all sorts of problems they did not want their families to suffer. So, while they would puff on the cigarette, they would talk to themselves and remind themselves that they were righteous, pure, holy, and sanctified. They would tell themselves that their identity was not in the cigarette. What happened with everyone who applied these principles faithfully in this manner, was that the power of nicotine lost its strength and the desire to smoke eventually fell away.

I have witnessed the same with others who struggled with pornography. In the midst of their struggle to get free, on every occasion that they gave in to the lust, they would remind themselves that they were righteous, that they were loved of God, and that this bondage was not who they were. It did not take long until the grace, or God's ability, would take root in their heart until there was no more "need" for the pornography to fulfill an unrealistic fantasy.

The basic principle is to address the addiction, sense of lack, habits, mindset, or whatever and deal with it at the heart. Ask yourself why you feel you need that thing or why you believe contrary to God's Word and then let the Holy Spirit speak back to your heart. Once He gives the answers, simply deal with it through the filters of *righteousness*, *grace*, and *hope*. You may not receive 100 percent freedom the first time, but you will begin to greatly weaken sin's hold over you. When you are under grace, sin will have no dominion over you (Romans 6:14). Those who struggle with sin simply are not fully established in grace. Praise the Lord for His grace as you and I are gaining great ground by His ability flowing through us, and our images are reflecting more and more like Jesus.

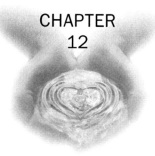

PERCEPTION: SEEING THROUGH THE EYES OF THE HEART

*Jesus said to her, "Did I not say to you that **if you would believe you would see the glory of God?**"*

John 11:40, emphasis added

We as sons and daughters of God have had our dominion on the earth restored to us through Jesus. We are to be the leaders and teachers of both physical and spiritual matters. We are to be caretakers and good stewards of the creation entrusted to us. Mankind is supposed to be highly sensitive to and aware of the spiritual realities as well as the physical, having our senses exercised so that we can appropriately discern good and evil. The question then must be asked, what happened?

Man was created in the likeness of God and was to function with greater ability than the animals. Man was given choice and the ability to change the environment he lived in as well as within himself. Furthermore, God created man to be in touch with and understand his own heart. Instinct is no exception.

Have you ever noticed how animals in the wild—and even those tamed by man—have an innate ability to just know how to live and function in the design they were intended for? An orphaned fawn, even if it was not yet weaned from its mother, will still know what plants are edible, poisonous, and even medicinal, all without the mother ever teaching it. Instinct is so powerful that it is the guidance system for migrating birds, which travel thousands of miles to return every year to the same nesting grounds. In addition, it is even more amazing that most migrate during the night. Even our domesticated pets seem to know what grasses to chew to soothe an upset stomach.

Moving further, this base instinct that animals function in have saved their own lives on numerous occasions. Take, for example, the tsunami of 2001. It was recorded that elephants, bats, birds, cats, and dogs were running into the hills and jungles the day the tsunami hit. Several dog owners who daily took their pets for a run on the beach reported their dogs refusing with great effort to go out that day. These animals knew something was wrong and responded to the feeling they had. How is it that these animals, which man is supposed to take care of and have "dominion" over, are better able to discern than man?

Using the example of instinct, an animal knows how to live from its heart. Yes, an animal too has a heart, just like man. In the book of Daniel, chapter 4, it says the watchers and holy ones said to the Lord that something must be done about King Nebuchadnezzar. It was their decree that Nebuchadnezzar be humbled, and God did so by removing the *heart* of a man and replacing it with the *heart* of an animal. By bringing up this example, it further proves the Word, which says our heart is the determining factor in what we live in life. The principle in action was the fact that after God changed Nebuchadnezzar's heart, his body responded and grew claws and feathers like hair to cover his human body. In addition, after his heart was changed, his body then was able to eat grass, which would have otherwise caused him to vomit and be malnourished. Just by changing the heart, the entire being transformed. Even science has proven that every cell in our body knows what we believe and will respond to that belief.

When God created all of creation and gave them instinct, did He forget about man? Of course not! Man too has instinct, but he has grown numb to the realities of heart and spirit. In essence, we often have dumbed ourselves down lower than our own animals. In our lusts for fulfillment from the false gods of the flesh, we have embraced our physical bodies and elevated the world of flesh—only to have thrown aside all spiritual practicality. Animals do not operate in magic or mysticism when they simply live by listening to their instinct through their heart. Neither should man think it strange to become familiar with the area of the heart.

Even science has proven that every cell in our body knows what we believe and will respond to that belief.

I also have witnessed on many instances an animal sense an evil presence. Once my sister's dog jumped up out of a dead sleep and stared in the corner of the room growling. She and I were talking on the phone at that moment, so I told her to command the spirit to leave and watch what would happen. When she did, the dog followed with her eyes from the corner of the room along the wall over to the big picture window and then shifted her focus outside. Once she was looking outside, the dog got aggressive and acted ferocious toward the demonic presence as it left. That stupid demon was just trying to bring in fear and confusion, but it was the dog that picked up the actual presence.

Please consider that I am not teaching on the difference between man and animals. There is clearly a difference between humans and animals. I am just pointing out some base similarities and functions of the heart for both man and animal alike. We are created in the likeness of God. It was man whom God personally breathed into to give life. We as mankind are the offspring of God. God crowned man with dignity and honor and then commanded him to have dominion in all the earth and sea. Unfortunately, man often has tried to walk in the dominion restored to us through Jesus without first establishing the dignity and honor. It is this dignity and honor that enable man to handle the responsibility of dominion on planet Earth.

There are several different scientific studies I have seen that said the same thing, but used different calculations to get different numbers. These studies have shown that there are approximately four million bits of information that bombard us every second of every day. However, the human brain can process only about two thousand bits of information per second. This means that nearly 3,998,000 bits of information are filtered out of our consciousness.

So what determines our filters? Our beliefs. Frankly, we will see what we believe. Literally, studies have shown that our beliefs determine what we will see; they determine our perception of the world around us. Those beliefs determine what we will allow into our conscious framework to perceive. I could talk about perception for days, but I want to try and keep it down to its basic simplistic form.

PERCEPTION

Then some of the Pharisees who were with Him heard these words, and said to Him, "Are we blind also?" Jesus said to them, "If you were blind, you would have no sin; but now you say, 'We see.' Therefore your sin remains."

John 9:40-41

Nearly all great successes come after someone quits insisting on how things are going to work. We have to come to a place in our lives where we accept "nothing is as *I* see it." Nothing out "there" is really the way "*I*" see it. Jesus said that what makes us blind is when we determine things truly are the way "*I*" see them to be through our interpretation. Saying that "I see" is the root of all blindness. The reason we cannot see the world the way it really is, is also the reason we cannot get out of the trap we are in. Our heart is also the vessel for perception. Everything we see with the physical eye is altered to match up with our beliefs. How we see it is not how it is; it is how *we* see it.

Everything we see with the physical eye
is altered to match up with our beliefs.

We need to get to a point where we yield to God and allow Him to lead us down the path He chooses. I must be willing to die to all of my selfish, self-centered, and self-promoting ways I think I need for quality of life. We all must quit insisting on how things should work based upon our own understanding. We must come to a place where we trust and believe what God says. Everything externally is viewed and interpreted through perception.

Allow me to share a quick example I once heard some time back. There was an island territory in which the islanders did not wear shoes. Two separate companies sent representatives to scout out potential sales for their products in this newer territory. One rep called back to his company and said, "Get me out of here. These people don't even wear shoes; we are wasting our time." The other rep called his company and said, "Get me everything you can afford to send. These people are not wearing any shoes; we have tremendous potential."

COMIC RELIEF

I want to interject some very comical, yet useful facts to illustrate perception. The following quotes are taken from a book entitled *Jolly Jokes for Older Folks*, by Bob Phillips.[1]

"Computers in the future may weigh no more than 1.5 tons."
Popular Mechanics, *forecasting the relentless march of science, 1949*

"I think there is a world market for maybe five computers."
Thomas Watson, chairman of IBM, 1943

"I have traveled the length and breadth of this country and talked with the best people, and I can assure you that data processing is a fad that won't last out a year."
The editor in charge of business books for Prentice Hall, 1957

"There is no reason anyone would want a computer in their home."
Ken Olson, president, chairman and founder of Digital Equipment Corp., 1977

---

1 Eugene, Oregon: Harvest House Publishers, 2007.

"This 'telephone' has too many shortcomings to be seriously considered as a means of communication. The device is inherently of no value to us."

Western Union internal memo, 1876

"I'm just glad it'll be Clark Gable who's falling on his face and not Gary Cooper."

Gary Cooper on his decision not to take the leading role in Gone With the Wind

"A cookie store is a bad idea. Besides, the market research reports say America likes crispy cookies, not soft and chewy cookies like you make."

Response to Debbie Fields' idea of starting a Mrs. Fields Cookies

"We don't like their sound, and guitar music is on the way out."

Decca Recording Co. rejecting the Beatles, 1962

"If I had thought about it, I wouldn't have done the experiment. The literature was full of examples that said you can't do this."

Spencer Silver on the work that led to the unique adhesives for 3M Post-it notepads

"So we went to Atari and said, 'Hey, we've got this amazing thing, even built with some of your parts, and what do you think about funding us? Or we'll give it to you. We just want to do it. Pay our salary, we'll come work for you.' And they said, 'No.' So then we went to Hewlett-Packard, and they said, 'Hey, we don't need you. You haven't got through college yet.'"

Apple Computer Inc. founder Steve Jobs on attempts to get Atari and H-P interested in his and Steve Wozniak's personal computer.

"Professor Goddard does not know the relation between action and reaction and the need to have something better than a vacuum against which to react. He seems to lack the basic knowledge ladled out daily in high schools."

New York Times *editorial about Robert Goddard's*
revolutionary rocket work, 1921

"Stocks have reached what looks like a permanently high plateau."

Irving Fisher, Professor of Economics, Yale University, 1929

"Everything that can be invented has been invented."

Charles H. Duell, Commissioner, U.S. Office of Patents, 1899

"Louis Pasteur's theory of germs is ridiculous fiction."

Pierre Pachet, Professor of Physiology at Toulouse, 1872

"The abdomen, the chest, and the brain will be forever shut from the intrusion of the wise and humane surgeon."

Sir John Eric Ericksen, British surgeon, appointed Surgeon-
Extraordinary to Queen Victoria, 1873

Here is another enlightening view on perspective. Joshua Bell is noted as one of the greatest musicians in the world. He played incognito at a metro station in Washington, D.C. It was organized by *The Washington Post* as a social experiment. In short, with a violin worth near $3.5 million, he played for nearly an hour one of the most intricate pieces ever written. After that hour there was $32 collected and only six people stopped and listened for a short time out of the approximate two thousand people who passed by. The $32 was collected from about twenty people who gave. The irony here is just two days prior, Joshua Bell sold out a theater in Boston with seats averaging $100 each.

Here is the thing. We all have an outlook or perspective on life. Our perceptions are based on our beliefs. So, in totality we are responsible for our own perception. We choose our own limits to the life we live. The comical and seemingly absurd statements from the quotations earlier listed are funny to consider, but the people who said some of those things were speaking from the perception they currently believed. To them, the limits were placed; there was no other way to see it. Wouldn't it be embarrassing if your or my name was listed as one of those making the comments above? However, truth be told, we all have made comments like these. I ask you, where are your limits with God today? Where are you limiting yourself or others to the abundant life Jesus said to live? Why settle for others' limitations? Those with creative capability are generally criticized by the masses to slow down and stop rocking the boat. It is divinely put in our DNA to be like our creative Father God, who inspires us to pursue the perception of hope, freedom, creativity, and belief. Jesus said we would do greater things than what He did because, after the work of the cross was finished, there would be limitless peace and access to our Father and inheritance in Him. So then, why do we continue to limit our perception to a lower standard?

THE STATES OF MIND

We discussed briefly the animal kingdom and how they live out of their instinct as a primary control. This is also true for children. When we are born, we are born operating one hundred percent on instinct. We are born into what the science community would call an alpha state of consciousness.

There are four basic states of consciousness in regards to the electrical impulses of the brain. We can operate from a beta, alpha, theta, or delta consciousness. Allow me to break these down into a very basic and broad explanation. Our brain works similar to a record player. It has electrical frequencies that are called brain waves. Brain waves make cycles every second. These states of consciousness are recorded in the brain wave activity.

A beta state is the most common state of mind for the "civilized" world; it is also the least productive. In the beta state your brain has cycles that range from 15 to 40 cycles per second. These cycles per second basically reveal the arousal of the logical brain. In alpha you range from 9 to 14 cycles per second. Theta is recorded at a proximity of 5 to 8 cycles, and delta ranges from 1.5 to 4 cycles per second.

The brain wave cycles merely signify the openness to receptivity and awareness. When we are consumed in external physical activities, we tend to put all of our attention on the physical attributes, calculating, analyzing, and defining the situation. This is what I often refer to as "tunnel vision." It is where we are focused or consumed with one thing. It is like a deep and well-worn rut where nothing seems to exist outside of that narrow center of attention. The beta state (tunnel vision) is when we are consumed with stress, logic, and circumstance, making decisions and determinations based upon the physical information alone. The beta state is the least healthy and the least creative.

Moving next into the alpha, we find our awareness heightened and creativity boosted. The alpha state significantly has less brain wave cycles; thus, the brain is capable of processing more clearly. There is less activity, resulting in the ability to process more outside information and creativity. Creativity is really looking at and considering common everyday information or things in new perspectives, yielding to new potentials or ideas. Alpha is considered one of the healthiest and most advantageous states. Children almost constantly live in the alpha state—that is, until we beat it out of them through vast amounts of education solely directed to the logic, and not balancing it with the spiritual counterparts. It is our design and to out benefit to live in the alpha. Children are extremely impressionable. They tend to sense things and feel things more than they logically reason. They learn more through conveyance than basic intellectual information. Children really don't have a healthy perspective because of the right information; it is more like healthy perspectives are a result of the way a child was made to feel.[2]

Consider this quote from Dr. James B. Richards as well:

> The top objective in parenting should be to make our children feel loved, accepted, and secure. In that environment, they will be trusting, teachable, and compliant. The goals for raising healthy children and pastoring healthy congregations should be the same. If the heart feels safe, it is open and teachable. If there is acceptance, then the reason for teaching is not perceived as rejection. People should never be taught because they are wrong, but because they are loved.[3]

---

2 See Dr. James B. Richards, *How to Stop the Pain* (New Kensington, Pennsylvania: Whitaker House, 2001), 80.

3 Ibid., 81.

Following in line of alpha is the theta state. Theta is a place of the slowest conscious brain frequency. Theta is the optimum creativity. In theta you learn things no one taught you. Yes, it is the place where the Bible refers to as the secret place of the heart. It is from theta that you can locate and function from the core of your heart. This is the state of deep meditation, a state where ideas flow the easiest and where deep contemplation takes place. Theta is the place of clarity in communication between you and the Lord. You know it as the place when you step in your "prayer closet" and spend quality time with God; it is where you slip into a place of silence and purity before Him. It is also the place where, after much time worshiping or time in prayer, you sense that clarity of connectedness. It is not that God decided to come visit; it is more the fact that you are now able to consciously be aware of His everabiding presence within you.

Finally, we arrive at the delta state. Delta is where we are unconscious or asleep. When we sleep without dreaming, we are in a deep state of delta. When we dream, our brain waves have increased and we are not in the deepest sleep. Whenever people go to bed, they turn out the light and go from beta to alpha to theta and finally to delta. Again, once they wake up, they go from a delta state to theta, alpha, and typically to beta. If people have trouble sleeping, for example, many times they are loaded down with stress and do not know how to get out of the beta state to relax and let go to enter the natural process of entering delta. (I will speak more about this "problem solving" in upcoming chapters about meditation: accessing the heart.)

Although one may have high frequencies say, in beta, there are always trace frequencies of alpha, theta, and delta at work. This is what science has discovered, and these are scientific explanations to a part of your human makeup. I wanted to bring up this awareness because I need you to understand some of where I am going and the language I will use as a reference.

ENTERING ALPHA

The alpha state is not difficult to enter by any means. In fact, you have done it on many occasions without necessarily being aware of it. An example of someone who slips into an alpha state would be someone who, after a conference, sits down to take a break or walks in a garden. It is that place of relaxation and letting go of the never-ending dialogue in your head. Your thoughts will still be with you, but they slow down greatly and become peaceful. This is alpha. Something else very neat about this place of alpha is the fact that it is like the razor's edge between beta and theta. Alpha is then an ideal position for awareness.

We are a duality. Man is part flesh and spirit. To live in alpha we are at the crossroad between the typical dominant logical mind and the pure mind of the spirit. Our logical minds are at once our greatest allies and our greatest enemies. If we can control the logical mind, it will serve as one of our greatest tools for incorporating the life of the spirit in the natural world. At the same time, we cannot live completely separate from our spiritual minds. To do so, we would be no good on planet Earth. If we get so spiritual that we neglect the physical realities, then we may as well leave and go home to heaven. There is much work for us here in the earth, and it is our job to bring heaven and earth together in our world and live in the balance of that oneness Jesus presented.

When you live in the alpha, you are able to open up your awareness beyond the physical five senses. You actually become aware of what much of the world would call a "sixth sense." If you allow yourself, you can pay attention to the subtle nuances and shifts within your heart. You can sense where you should or should not be placing your attention. In alpha you are capable of exercising your senses to sensitize your discernment. For example, you may be making plans for a family trip, but somehow you keep getting a negative feeling about it. Eventually, you decide to listen to that "gut feeling," cancel your plans, and the weekend you were supposed to be gone, you have a flood in your house. But, because you stayed home, you were able to salvage and save everything! This actually happened to Andrea and me. In the alpha state we were able to pick up the sense in our "gut" about something not right in regards to leaving for the trip.

In alpha you are able to switch over and use the beta reasoning; logical, mathematical abilities; or the theta spiritual aspect very easily. Even more importantly, you can use them both at the same time. What is really neat is that you can learn to work from logic and spirit simultaneously. Alpha makes it easier, no matter what the occasion demands, to increase your awareness and use the tools God has made available to you. Of course, you realize I am not talking about the spiritual tools only, but also the physical ones.

You can learn to work from logic and spirit simultaneously.

If you sit for five minutes in what I will call *wide angle vision*, you will find yourself in alpha. Getting to alpha is just the beginning. Learning to communicate, listen, work miracles, and live there is something we will get into later. Don't be intimidated; it is much easier than many would make it out to be. In fact, living from this place is a very natural and comforting feeling. The reason being, it is where you were created and designed to live from.

Wide angle vision is nothing more than looking through your full peripheral, meaning all of your senses at once. If you stand, sit, play, or work, you easily can slip into a high state alpha and even theta. (Either of these can be called *wide angle vision*; they just have different depths of sensitivity.) But, first let's start with the alpha. Now to practice, sit and relax for five minutes. When you do so, with your eyes open, look at the entire horizon. See the sky and ground; take in the whole picture as a whole. Do not focus directly on one spot. Make sure you just absorb everything like a thirsty sponge. Do the same with your senses of hearing, touch, taste, and smell. Don't forget to include taking in the feelings through your heart as well. This is *wide angle vision*. Do not try to focus in on one thing; rather, let everything absorb without describing or zeroing in on any one thing. Again, do not try to describe or think about what you are taking in. Just be. Allow your senses to reach out and experience everything effortlessly without analyzing with thoughts. It is like thoughtlessly allowing all of your senses to imprint on your soul, letting go of your lust to analyze and define. Don't think an emotion—feel the emotion.

Imagine coming home from a very long and hard day of work. You walk into your living room and sit in your favorite chair. Maybe it is a comfortable recliner—you sit down to relax with the leg rest up. As you lean back, you let out a deep sigh, effortlessly letting go all of the stress from the day's responsibilities. As you sat back and surrendered all stress with that deep sigh, you were shifting from a beta to an alpha state. Do you ever notice how children naturally live carefree? It is because they live in an alpha state until approximately ages 8 to 12, depending on their environment. God's design for man was not to live from the vacuum of flesh in the beta, laboring under the physical stress and cares of this world. That is why Jesus commanded you and I to fling our cares upon Him! It is our job to maintain that peace and rest in Him.

CHANGE OF PERCEPTION

What you will begin to notice, as you make the decision to slow down and take into consideration the underlying nuances and shifts within your heart, is a whole new world emerging. These nuances and nearly subconscious feelings are very subtle, which is why the Bible calls the voice of the Lord the "still small voice." I even refer to the voice of the Holy Spirit as the "voiceless voice of the Holy Spirit." In upcoming chapters I will get more into the language and communication of heart, but for now I want to put your attention on opening your eyes to perceiving the unseen and eternal.

I don't want to get anyone hung up on manufacturing emotions at all. Howbeit, we all have emotions, and those emotions tend to lead our lives. To a large degree, we live based upon our emotions. I know this does not sound well in certain Christian circles, but it is still the truth. We tend to say, "I don't live by my emotions; I live by faith. 'As many as are the sons of God are led by the Spirit of God.' So, I don't follow my emotions, I tell my emotions how to feel." This is true, but the emotions will still direct our actions. We may tell our emotions how to feel, and once they feel the way we order them to, we then follow and effortlessly live the direction they are taking us. The only issue is we need to keep a constant check on where they are leading us. That is done, however, through our thoughts and even more accurately said, beliefs. The Bible says that man is a "living soul." Because we are a living soul, it is good that we have emotions. It is our design to be a people of passion and feelings. We just need to guard those feelings and learn the skillfulness of controlling and mastering our soul to prosper instead of neglecting our soul, which leads to us destroying ourselves.

To a large degree,
we live based upon our emotions.

The alpha state (wide angle vision) is a place where it is easiest to maintain the necessary inner awareness. From this place of awareness, we can pay attention to what we normally would not pay attention to. I often have said, "Give attention to what you aren't paying attention to." What I mean by this is to simply know yourself. Ask yourself, "Why did I take this way home from work?" "How am I feeling?" "How does this make me feel?" "What is this teaching me?"

The point is not to ask yourself a bunch of questions; the point is rather to feel what is going on inside of you and then to know the "why." If you were to live in the prison of flesh through the beta state (tunnel vision), you would be limited to the five physical senses. Beta is an intellectual state of existence. It is a prison that will not yield to the spiritual self, much less to the spiritual perception of the world around you. There are so many people solely existing in a lifeless material world. They are among the living dead. They have no purpose, no vision. The mindless grey masses of society are living in a vacuum absorbed with the false gods of flesh as their only safety, security, and comfort.

BECOME A CHILD AGAIN

And said, "Assuredly, I say to you, unless you are converted and become as
little children, you will by no means enter the kingdom of heaven."
                                                                Matthew 18:3

As adults, most of us have lost the ability to enter and live from the alpha state. This is often why people who have had a lifetime of particular teaching or beliefs experience great difficulty or hardness in embracing and learning new dynamics of truth and greater dimensions of the life of God. Whereas, children, who for the most part live in alpha, are highly impressionable in their young years because they live more out of the heart realm. To live out of the "alpha," there must be a degree of surrender. What I mean by surrender is a surrender of ego, logic, and lust to define. Do you think Jesus may have been referring to this impressionable sensitivity of the heart when He said we must become as children? I wholeheartedly do believe that Jesus was referring to a child's impressionability and tenderness to receive and learn from the world around him or her. We once again are to soften our heart to be like a child's to allow the Lord to become our influence and source for shaping our new heart in Him. In fact, as adults we for the most part live from a heart that was formed when we were impressionable children, but our logical reasoning is trained to think as adults. Our minds, or reasoning, interpret much of our external circumstances through the subconscious heart beliefs formed when we were children. No one can enter the realm of the Kingdom by means of his or her ego, pride, selfish motivation, or personal perception.

Blessed are the pure in heart: for they shall see God.
                                              Matthew 5:8 KJV

Living from the heart will never work unless one has integrity of heart. If your objective is to justify yourself, your emotions, or your opinions, then you only will pollute your heart further by imposing false perceptions and crooked judgments that line up with what you *want* God to tell you. The reason those who are pure in heart will see God is because they are not distorting truth. They have no ulterior motivation or selfish ambition, other than to know and walk with God. They are those who seek God in truth. That means they want to live truth and not their traditions or personal philosophies. They are teachable and willing to change their current perspective to follow after truth in its purity. Because of their purity, they will see God for who He truly is, and not according to their skewed perceptions of preconceived ideas. Those who are pure in heart are willing to release their old perspectives and allow God to bring change and truth, even if they are contrary to cultural traditions.

Yes, we are at this point becoming vulnerable. In spite of the pain and harm done toward us in the past by others, the only road to freedom is to open our heart to Jesus and yield ourselves fully to Him and His Word, just as an infant or toddler does with his or her parent. The fear is from the hurt our heart tries to protect us from in opening ourselves to that degree of vulnerability, which once cost us so much pain in the past. Walking in the Kingdom of God with this type of purity demands absolute surrender and trust.

Then Jesus answered and said to them, "Most assuredly, I say to you, the Son can do nothing of Himself, but what He sees the Father do; for whatever He does, the Son also does in like manner."

John 5:19

Most of us read this and think Jesus had some superhuman ability to look into heaven with a special pair of binoculars. The word Jesus used to describe "seeing" what the Father was doing is the Greek word *blepo*. *Blepo* translates to the word *perceive*.[4] Often scripture would say Jesus *perceived* the thoughts or reasonings of so and so. Really, Jesus was in touch with and sensitive to His heart. He even said that at one time He *perceived* healing power go out of Him when walking down the street in the middle of a mob. This is not a superhuman ability; it is an expansion of consciousness to be aware beyond the five physical senses.

Jesus revealed a powerful understanding here. Herein is that truth: Everyone conducts his or her life and ministry exactly as he or she perceives God. Do you perceive an angry god? Then you are an angry preacher and family man. Do you have a generous and kind God? Then, you are a generous and merciful preacher and family man. Jesus said He did only what He perceived the Father doing. In the beginning, developing your perception may sound complex and difficult, but by the end of this study it will come full circle to something so simple that it is almost hard to describe other than to do it.

---

4 James Strong, *The Exhaustive Concordance of the Bible* (Nashville, Tennessee: Holman Bible Publishers, n.d.), #G991.

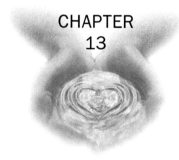

MEDITATION: CONCENTRATION POINTS

*L*et's be very clear right from the beginning. You picked up this book, I hope, because you wanted to better understand the heart. In order to understand it, you must be willing to look at your own heart. It is here in the beginning of this chapter that you must lay down your prejudices and opinions that for far too long have imprisoned you in the world of flesh, blinding you from the dynamic spiritual life you have been missing. I am very aware that when you begin to examine your heart, you may find things in there that you don't like. Don't be alarmed! Your heart will never give you more to deal with than you can handle.

In addition, I am sure that just using the word *meditation* will offend some. Personally, I too hate the word *meditation*. That word has been perverted by our society and completely distorted into some mystical idea of sitting and feeling beyond ourselves with no real purpose. Instead of being a bridge, meditation has become a prison. Although it is true we will be able to perceive to a certain degree spiritually, many think that is the end result. Contemporary understanding of meditation for the most part is use-less. Most modern meditation has no power. Because of these things, many Christians have feared what they have not understood and, so doing, tried to do away with "meditation" altogether. Howbeit, without meditation, Christianity has no spiritual existence on planet Earth.

MEDITATION IS...

First, we must address the question, why meditation? It is so we can conceptualize that particular truth; it is so we can grasp the idea in order to receive the truth of God in our heart. Unless we can see the truth of God's promise or His Word personalized and working in and thru us, or see ourselves as God sees us, our heart cannot embrace the truth of it. If a truth is foreign to us, we cannot get it into our heart. We have to get it in our heart experientially through meditation. This is why testimonies are so powerful. They allow us to see how a truth came alive and transformed someone else's life—and then we can conceptualize and see that truth working in our own life.

To make a very basic point, had you not "meditated," you would not have been able to believe and receive Jesus in your life. Think about it. You heard someone teaching about the Christ, you then perceived in your heart that it was true, which lead you to believe, which changed your feelings, and ultimately your actions to confess and receive. The simple fact that you were able to perceive through the heart says that to some degree you were in that alpha state with the ability to access your heart through pondering or contemplating the words you heard or read. The Bible further commands you and I to live our life in the same way we first believed: "As you therefore have received Christ Jesus the Lord, so walk in Him" (Colossians 2:6).

Had you not "meditated," you would not have been able to believe and receive Jesus in your life.

I made mention in a preceding chapter of the beta state of mind. Let me further clarify what this beta state really is. Beta is another way for me to explain the world of the "living dead." Like I stated previously, this is the state in which most of mankind is imprisoned in today. It is a world of flesh, of logical thought, where the intellect and physical are the only reality, the only god. Most of mankind cannot escape from this coffin of flesh—not because they do not know how, but because that is where the physical mind feels safe. Due to the overindulgence of the physical mind, many have completely neglected the spiritual. Thus their spiritual minds have gone into atrophy. Man living in the prison of flesh is not really living at all.

The Bible is full of examples of meditation. I gave examples of meditation in my first book of this spiritual field guide series. Words such as *ponder, consider, commune, think upon, imagination, meditate, muse,* and *pray* are all meditative words. These words are concepts that much of Westernized modern man struggles to understand the value of. We want the fast, big, explosive, entertaining, and rush of life, but we go about finding it through physical means. Today few find rapture in considering the heavens, as the psalmist put it. Or how about gazing at the ant and feeling the significance of its life and learning the lessons it has to teach? Plants too are no exception. Mankind's ego is so top heavy that he is blinded to the wonders and miracles of life that exist all around him. The Bible also teaches us that all of the attributes of God can be learned by studying creation. That concept alone is confounding to our logical, egotistical society.

Understand that everyday people "meditate" and don't even realize it. When you drive home and are in deep contemplation, you actually at some degree are meditating on that "thing." Whatever it is you are contemplating, that "thing" has become the concentration point; you are meditating within your heart and searching out the matter. That is only one example of thousands. I even remember once while playing sports slipping into a deep unconscious meditation. It was completely by accident and up until about seven years ago I did not understand what took place that day.

I was at a wrestling meet, which was my first year wrestling in the eighth grade of junior high school. My opponent was a state wrestler and to say he was better than I would have been a tremendous understatement. Further, it was my first year in public school from being homeschooled. I was intimidated and insecure in my new surroundings as well as in the new sport. I wanted nothing more than to beat this guy. When I went out on the mat, it was merely a cat and mouse game, with me as the mouse. My coach even told me not to take this to heart, for this kid had been wrestling since the age of five or six years old. All I remember after the first period was that I did not want to lose. I didn't know what I was doing except for two or three moves, and my adrenaline was pumping like crazy. I remember starting the next period, and that was it. The next memory I have after that was the referee holding up my arm as I won! I walked away and thought I was going crazy. I couldn't remember the entire match. I literally thought I needed hospitalization. Apparently I used the couple moves I knew and just kept doing those and won the match by points. It was the fact that I lost consciousness yet still won the match that scared the tar out of me for years. What actually took place, as I understand today, was that I was so determined and single-mindedly focused that all else disappeared and I accidentally let go into a deep theta state where my instincts took complete control. To say it frankly, I slipped into a profound and powerful meditation. This is the same state you hear of when women rip car doors off to save their children inside after an accident. That adrenaline mixed with the surrender of limiting thought is what some cultures would call releasing the animal within. It serves also as a self-preservation mechanism, used in dire situations.

I am not writing a book to convince you of the power of meditation; rather, this is a how-to tome. If you need persuasion regarding meditation, you can look in your Bible and do a search on the Hebrew words *siychah* and *siyach*. These words are conceptual words of what we would call meditation today.

Meditation in its basic element is when you decide to access your heart. Meditation in simplicity is deep contemplative thought from a relaxed and focused state. Now, that is a broad explanation, but let's keep things simple for now. I am going to deal with meditation that concerns you and your personal journey in Christ, the hope of glory *in* you. Meditation, or contemplation, is nothing more than the practice of utilizing your entire being. Through meditation you incorporate your spirit, soul, and body and open yourself up to the influence of the Holy Spirit to freely work through you, instead of solely relying on the dominant physical mind. You always are using your soul in life, but through meditation you can harness the power of the soul and use it to work with your spirit and live a complete life in the material world. It is through this meditation process that you can reclaim your soul and make it line up with the Word of God in thought, feeling, and emotion. Meditation allows you to see beyond the façade.

Meditation allows you to see beyond the façade.

Like all things, meditation can be perverted, abused, and used for evil. As with any thing, meditation is not inherently good or evil; it is how a person purposes to use it. Remember, I am not referring to a useless meditation that has no purpose or that cannot work while at play, work, worship, or family time. I am talking about a powerful dynamic meditation that, with little time, anyone can eventually develop and successfully live in. Meditation is a tool; your purpose and motivation are what determine whether the meditation will be used for Godly measures or not. The point being, any time you have lusted, envied, hated, lied, and so forth, you engaged in the meditative process. And unless there was a change of mind (repentance), you strengthened your heart in those areas to some degree. On the other hand, Philippians 4:8 says, "Finally, brethren, whatever things are true, whatever things are noble, whatever things are just, whatever things are pure, whatever things are lovely, whatever things are of good report, if there is any virtue and if there is anything praiseworthy—meditate on these things."

Never, ever, allow someone to lead you in a meditation unless you know him or her well and unless the purpose is for healing or wholeness. No one can take away control from you without your giving it to them. You decide whether or not to relinquish control. You are always in control of that decision.

The greatest meditation is to live it. In the beginning of understanding the heart and spiritual principles, it is good to consciously go within and examine your heart. Eventually, you should get to a place where you live in that state. The state I am speaking of is the alpha state I mentioned previously. Meditation is not an optimal benefit unless it is a lifestyle: a waking, walking, dynamic meditation. Yes, what I am talking about is living a lifestyle from the heart. I am referring to a life that always is aware of the heart, is in communication with the Lord, has an abiding sense of His presence, and is sensitive to the greater realities beyond flesh.

In the beginning it may sound farfetched to believe one can live a life from the heart. However, we did once before naturally as children. We all crave to know and perceive beyond the intellectual realm. All humans have an innate sense—the God DNA—that tells us there is more to life than the material things we put so much emphasis on. This meditation I have been speaking of is the bridge, the pathway, to the spiritual mind. Once the spiritual mind is presented, we can then use it in harmony with our logical mind. Really, the only time the logical mind is our enemy is when it hinders us from accessing our pure minds of the spirit. Of course, one serves its purpose in the physical, the other in the spirit; together we work as a complete person.

Again, I must emphasize the fact that it is much easier than it sounds. You were designed by God to live in this state. Don't be intimidated, as I said before. Throughout your life you have functioned from your spiritual mind many times. I just want to establish a foundation so you know the tools for living from the heart.

As we begin to discuss biblical meditation, I want to make sure we do not complicate things. Many of us have walked very close to the Lord and have been people living from the heart already. I just want to break down some of the normal processes we go through when dealing with the heart. My desire is not to take away our focus from Jesus at all! It is to empower our walk and clarity with Him. We must keep things simple!

There is power in simplicity. In the beginning here, my explanation of things may seem a little complex. Just understand that I am going to delve into the inner workings of our heart, but in the end we always will bring things back to the simplicity of Christ and our identity in Him. The goal here is to help sensitize our awareness of who we are and to become aware of the heart realm. I also desire to help sharpen our ability to perceive and live in the balance of flesh and spirit. Our ultimate goal is to know Jesus intimately and the power outflowing from His resurrection.

THE FOUR ELEMENTS OF MEDITATION

There are spiritual laws and principles that we live by. There are also principles to meditation. If we were to take the time to investigate the simplistic breakdown of meditation, we would find four basic elements. First, there must be comfort; second, there must be physical and mental relaxation. Third, there must be a passive attitude so that no outside distractions will interfere with the one meditating. Finally, there must be an absolute concentration point, something that focuses the physical mind in such a way that it ultimately quiets down and allows the purity of the spiritual mind to become clear and dominant.

Allow me to better explain the concentration point, which focuses the physical mind in a way to take control of it. You are both flesh and spirit. You have a physical body and a spiritual body. So too do you have a physical mind and a spiritual mind. As I made mention before, you also *have* a heart. Your heart is the seat of your beliefs and emotions; thus, it determines your perception in everyday life. You determine whether you will choose to be aware of what is going on internally or to stay focused only on the five physical senses. Your physical and spiritual minds are like two siblings fighting for dominance over one another. Due to the society you and I live in, it is often the logical mind that has complete control and squelches one's spiritual existence.

...I commune with mine own heart: and my spirit made diligent search.
Psalm 77:6 KJV

When we become heart conscious, our spirit will search out what has been written on the tablet of our heart, whether by ourselves or by others we allowed to write on our heart. Many times the Holy Spirit will reveal things to us in order to help walk us into wholeness and freedom. Now, let's not get hung up splitting hairs over whether it is our own spirit or the Holy Spirit revealing things. Our righteous spirit is one with Jesus' and our spirit is working in line with Jesus. As a hint, though, the more we practice, the better we will get at identifying between the two. We should begin to notice that when the Holy Spirit speaks, it is more authoritative. Also, the more we get used to communicating with the Holy Spirit, the more we will notice His personality difference from our own. We don't have to be preoccupied with wondering if our spirit will mislead us. Depending upon what we are writing on the tablet of our heart, the heart can mislead us, but our righteous spirit man will not.

That is why we need to learn to allow the peace of God to rule, or be the umpire of, our heart. We do not want the logical mind to be what persuades our heart. (More on this in Chapter 15.)

The term "pacifier" is what I will use to refer to what I made mention of as concentration points. We must learn to live in balance between the physical and spiritual worlds. It is learning to live within both worlds at the same time. Many of us have walked that "razor's edge" but perhaps lacked the terminology to describe how to "get there." That "there" is the place of the heart. The pacifier, or crutch, is a tool we sometimes may use to reduce the over-dominance of the physical mind. We might say it helps us quiet the mind and "bring it under control" so that the spiritual self is then able to be heard through the heart. It is also a way to find a place where the world comes to a stop, so to speak. Because of our fast-paced and hectic lifestyles, it is nearly a lost concept to commune within our heart and allow our spirit to make diligent search like David talked about.

As an illustration, you almost can picture your logical mind as a very loud baby who is screaming at the top of his lungs to be heard, to be the center of attention. When you need to hear the voice of your heart that is quietly speaking something to you, it becomes very difficult, if not impossible, to hear as long as the baby (your logical mind) keeps screaming to be heard at every moment. If you are a parent, you know that the easiest way to quiet the baby is with a pacifier. A pacifier is something you would give the baby that would help it to calm and quiet down so that you could finally hear the other voice in the room.

There are varying degrees of meditation. Everyone meditates to some level or another; it is just that not everyone knows what to do once there. Driving home from work and contemplating the day, relaxing after a long day and unwinding, daydreaming, being introspective, and so on, are some examples of meditating. Granted, these forms are unrestrained and lack depth; however, they are very much an introduction to meditation.

Not all children are pacified by the same toys. Nor is everyone's logical mind quieted by the same things. For some people, the pacifier maybe a place such as a prayer closet or a cathedral. By just being in the ambiance of a sug-gested holy structure, many are able to quiet the logical mind and allow the spiritual self to surface. While their logical mind is occupied with the presence of a structure or sacred place, they can allow their attention to focus on their heart. Others are able to quiet the physical mind by walking in nature. Yet others may prefer to sing a song that has significance to them, pray a familiar prayer, or do any other thing that will induce calmness and clarity of mind. It is like doing two things at once. It's almost like the way a melody in a song allows you to drift with the flow of its current. But while your mind is hearing the music, you become sensitive to the feelings and thoughts that have been waiting to emerge from your own heart. Or, using the example of nature, your mind can drift and flow with the calming rhythms of creation, allowing you to let go of the stress and pressures and thus allowing you to gain composure and clarity within. You may find yourself pondering and daydreaming about things that needed attention from a state of peace and clarity. In both of these examples, music and nature served as external pacifiers for the logical mind.

Everyone meditates to some level or another;
it is just that not everyone knows what to do once there.

Please hear the message of what I am saying. In no way am I saying that our methods of worship are superficial. We are commanded to worship God from the truth of our heart. I am simply differentiating between the melody of music and worship. Music can be a form of worship; it can be used to express worship, but worship is always from the heart. When we worship God using music, it is very real and powerful. The music actually helps us to empower our worship. Music can be an incredible tool to praise and worship God with. I just am trying to take us to a place where we are mature enough to not have to rely on a song to bring us into intimate worship. For example, if I have a laborious and stressful day of work and family life on Monday, I don't want to have to wait until Sunday to come back into the refreshing presence of God again. There are many occasions where we need to escape into the arms of the Father. Those who do not know how to find that peace and joy in God often turn to other things, such as drugs, to ease their pain.

Let me take music a little further with this topic. I personally am not musically inclined, and once I asked my friend why he enjoyed going to some of the bizarre concerts that had the head banging and raves. He quickly responded that it was a way for him to release all of the rage or emotion he had. He said he was able to let go, feel the music, and shed all of the stress, chaos, and burdens of life. The only problem with this was his limitation to the short-lived, external crutch, or pacifier, for release. You see, those types of concerts are one way for the world to "lighten the load" and release their emotions, but it is only a Band-aid method to a bigger problem.

Now, take music in a church setting. There have been occasions where praise music is not as much for God as it is for the people. It conditions the people to hear the Word of God. The music allows people to surrender and let their spiritual mind wake up and focus on God, on His presence, and esteem Him. There are instances where people do not feel that they can praise or worship God without music. The reason for this is that they rely on a praise and worship band as their crutch, or pacifier, to quiet the physical mind, due to various heart beliefs. Am I saying that praise and worship music is bad? Of course not! There is power in music that worships God. However, it is not the stroke of a stringed instrument or a thump of a drum that gives music the power. No, the power of music comes from the heart and spirit of the worshiper. The Lord inhabits that praise; it is a form of intimacy with us and Him. Remember the story I told in Volume 1, *How to Release the Power of Faith*, of the time I had a demon as a child? The only thing that calmed me and took away the pain of the evil spirit was when my mom played the piano to the Lord in sincere worship. A week later when she realized I was not just sick but had a demon, she cast it out.

Music is very good and beneficial, but we must grow into a mature people who can transcend the need of these pacifiers and worship God out of the purity of our heart in any situation or environment. Pacifiers, or crutches, are good to teach us and help us to locate and identify the heart zone, but in time we must learn to wean off of them. Don't misunderstand me; worship is many things besides a quieter of our logical mind. Those things always will be needed. When I say "wean ourselves" off these crutches, I mean that we should strive to be able to be heart conscious even without something external to help us quiet the logical mind. When I am faced with a difficult decision that could have drastic effects in either direction, I use every crutch

I can to quiet my logical reasoning in order to hear clearly the guidance of the Holy Spirit. My main pacifier is to escape into the wilderness places and have alone time in the temples of creation. I am merely pointing to a problem with today's meditation (heart consciousness), not only with the countless pacifiers, but also primarily with the fact that, in many cases, it has become very sedentary and unusable.

Many who read this may not have difficulty with accessing the heart. Thus our uses of pacifiers or crutches may seem obscure. Bear with me, as I am beginning to build a road map to walk in the simplicity of a daily dynamic living meditation, or heart awareness. If I can explain the process in logical terms, then those who struggle to understand and enter should find it easier to accept. It is our inspiration to know God and develop a trusting relationship with Him more than just know intellectual facts about Him. Having the Spirit of God within us, we ought to feel His thoughts and feelings. After all, you and He are one.

In various situations throughout the day, put your attention on Him and how He is feeling. It is possible; let your life become a state of prayer instead of praying only ten minutes a day. Live the prayer. I only point out those things about the pacifiers for self-awareness in order that you might push beyond the limitations you create and walk and talk with God whenever you choose. Ultimately, it is your choice to decide whether or not to live in communication with the Spirit (2 Corinthians 13:14).

Let your life become a state of prayer instead of praying only ten minutes a day. Live the prayer.

MEDITATION: ACCESSING THE HEART

AN INTRODUCTION TO THE SECRET PLACE

*N*ow that I have introduced the concept of meditation, I will continue to use the word *meditation*, even though I really have a dislike for the word. I trust that you will use the understanding of the new description of *accessing the heart* or *heart work* as a proper definition. Meditation in itself is not good or bad; it is more what your purpose is and what you do with it. There is nothing wrong with understanding and becoming strategic in using the internal senses God equipped us with. "But solid food belongs to those who are of full age, that is, those who by reason of use have their senses exercised to discern both good and evil" (Hebrews 5:14).

If we preach and teach things we do not live or understand, then we are setting ourselves up for disaster. I have had many instruct me solely based on their personal fears of the unknown. It is nothing more than a cultural battle. Because our culture is the intellectual powerhouse of Western society, we have tended to disregard any spiritual or heart understanding. The principles I am introducing are simple spiritual laws; we decide what we will do with them. It is not unlike the laws of electricity. An electrician can learn how electricity works, functions, and reacts, but it is up to him to decide what he will do with that knowledge. Once he learns how to operate within those laws, he can create all manner of benefits for his life and others because he has learned to effectively harness the power of electricity.

So too should we know ourselves in that way. We have been blessed greatly by God to be created in His likeness. It is not weird or mystical to be like Him. By learning the biblical laws of meditation, we can learn to use meditation to our benefit and the benefit of others. The psalmist wrote in Psalm 4:4, "...Meditate within your heart on your bed, and be still." There is great untapped potential that many Christians have overlooked in the Word of God by not understanding these prevailing truths about the power of meditation and how to use it. Conversely, there have been many who have walked this supernatural lifestyle but who lacked the words to define what was so natural for them to flow in due to their gifting.

I believe it is no accident that Isaac was recorded as meditating in the field during the evening (Genesis 24:63), or that Jesus was recorded as going out in the early morning to spend alone time with God (Mark 1:35). Studies have now shown, as we have briefly discussed, that the morning and the evening are when we tend to slip into a high alpha state. Even in the morning when I wake up, I often lie in bed for ten minutes pondering the day and the events that lie ahead. In the evenings I frequently lie in bed and ponder on the day's events and think on the course of the day. The wisdom in taking the first and last part of the day to meditate is to take advantage of the time when we are more easily yielded to the Holy Spirit and surrender the fast-paced logic of the mind. Using the morning for taking devotional time is the best because your physical mind is still trying to kick in gear and you are more capable of tuning in to your spiritual mind. Nonetheless, you can teach yourself how to recognize when you are in the beta, alpha, or theta state of mind. Also, you can teach yourself to be at peace and live in alpha as a conscious choice.

Remember how I earlier stated that when we are asleep we are in a delta state? Then, as we wake up, we go from a delta, to a theta, then to an alpha, and often to full beta. The cycle repeats itself as we go to sleep, from beta all the way down to delta. This being so, it is to our advantage to use the first and last part of our days as our time for deep meditation and introspection. For the most part, just as you wake up and about a half hour before you go to bed, you are at your alpha or theta state of awareness. It is then that I encourage you to do most of your heart work.

CREATING THE HEART ANCHOR

The four basic elements of meditation are comfort, physical and mental relaxation, a passive attitude (so that no outside distractions will interfere with the one meditating), and the absolute concentration point. I already dealt with the passive attitude that overcomes distractions in Volume 1. This attitude is achieved by believing so firmly that nothing can distract you from the task at hand, including heart work. The other two, comfort and relaxation, are internal states more than anything else. When you play, work, or do any other activity, are you not comfortable and relaxed? Yes, there may be physical exertion, but you still can be at peace inwardly to overcome the external pressures. So, now it is just a matter of what you put your attention on that matters.

I mentioned that pacifiers, or crutches, are not bad. We are to use the various crutches or pacifiers in the beginning to access the heart realm, then to become proficient to a point where we no longer *need* the pacifier to walk within the abiding presence of our Father or when working within our own heart. The crutch first helps us to locate and identify the heart; then from there we are able to landmark that internal state of peace. In the beginning, we use external crutches or pacifiers to help us control and quiet our physical minds. For example, in the early morning or evening as we meditate within our heart, we may need to play some praise and worship music softly to help us locate that place of peace and awareness of the Lord. Eventually, we need to learn to wean off of the external pacifiers and create internal ones. We should be able to enter the Kingdom of God within us anytime and anywhere with or without music or time of day. That does not mean we abandon those crutches, which help bring us to a place of surrender; they always will serve as a tool to bring us close to our Lord for whom our bodies are the temples. I am encouraging to rather become skillful with the things of the Spirit.

We all need to learn how to identify the heart zone, and even more importantly how to access our heart in depth whenever needed. First, we must learn to identify that "secret place" within. Whether we are at home praying, meditating on His Word, praising and worshiping, or fasting, and we begin to sense a deep and powerful presence of God, we have just accessed the secret place within the heart zone. It is very important to learn to identify this place for ourselves so that we can return there in the future. Everyone is different; we all have different ways we encounter or stir ourselves up to enjoy the presence of our Father and communion of the Spirit. So too are there different descriptions for how people would describe that secret place where the presence of the Lord is within.

You also may remember one of the exercises from Volume 1, which was to remember and write down every miracle from your life since your earliest memories. I did this to help identify that place of faith. In that exercise you actually were meditating and reliving various miraculous events from your life. In so doing, you were reestablishing what it felt like from that place of faith. Thus, you would become comfortable and know what it was to live from that state of being. In all actuality, you were accessing your heart.

God is always with us; it is just to what degree we are aware of His presence. Even in the midst of the debauchery of Las Vegas, for instance, God's presence is still there (Romans 5:20). We can experience the life and presence of God in us anytime we choose. Once we find ourselves in the emotion and feeling of that place of peace and rest, it is then that we create the heart *trigger*. This trigger will serve as an association to this place of the heart in order to help us to return to that place of peace, rest, safety, comfort, and encouragement anytime desired.

We can experience the life and presence
of God in us anytime we choose.

Now, you cannot create this anchor unless you are creating it from a place of a deep state of peace. The more real and powerful the meditation, the stronger the trigger can be made from there. In other words, you are creating a memory associated with an action. The memory is what you are experiencing from your meditation, or powerful imagination. Once you become conscious and feel the emotion and the peace and rest, then do something that will serve to associate that heart zone with the action. For example, when I am at a place of deep meditation in my heart and listening and talking with the Lord, I simply take a deep breath and exhale. The exhale serves as an association (an internal crutch) for me to find that place of deep meditation and awareness within. So, if I find myself in a high stress environment or in a position where there is confusion all around me, I just have to take a deep breath and, on the exhale, I surrender all my anxiety, stress, pain, tension, and sense of self with absolute belief to reenter that deep state of peace, love, joy, rest, quietness, and awareness of His presence. Then, from the state of peace, I am able to find His strength and ability during the time of need. The exhale is linked to the memory of the past experiences I have had, so it serves to help me locate that secret place deep in the core of my heart.

We can do anything to create an association as a heart anchor. I would suggest even playing a praise CD, but the problem with that is that we are not always able to pop in a CD and play the desired song. This is why the trigger I am suggesting become an internal one—one that then will serve as an internal crutch when needed. Jesus said we can approach His throne of grace in times of need. Why then is it that more Christians find it difficult to approach His throne? The answer goes back to the overindulgence and reliance on the intellect alone. There are a vast amount of Christians who do not know the heart as familiar territory. This is why we are going through the step of creating a heart trigger that will serve to associate the landmark of His abiding presence within.

Once you have accessed your heart zone, you possibly could say a word that has significance to you or maybe say the name of Jesus when there in His presence. The point is to do whatever feels right for you. Just do this action a couple times while in that deep heart-conscious state. Then, with a little time, it will serve to act as a trigger to launch you back to the desired location of the heart. You will have to strengthen the trigger from time to time in order to use it as an association during high stress times.

With time you will notice that there is no longer a need for an external or internal crutch to help you get to the heart zone. The exhale for me is a way to carry an internal pacifier. If you have not guessed, the heart anchor I am trying to help you create is an internal pacifier so you no longer need external environments or conditions to locate the place of heart. *In a short amount of time beyond this, all you will need is your choice. You will become so familiar with the heart that you will be able to access the riches of the life within you by merely making a decision to.*

THE LANGUAGE OF THE HEART

Accessing the heart is one thing; living from there and communicating from the heart is another. Although God occasionally does so, He does not primarily speak to us through external measures. He speaks to us through our heart. There are countless scriptures that reveal God's speaking to His children through the internal heart. First John 2:20 (KJV) says that we have an unction from the Holy One. This is like having an impression about something. The world describes it as a gut feeling, a hunch, a premonition, or even a sixth sense. All of those phrases work. Ultimately, the language of the heart is as follows: signs, symbols, visions, dreams, feelings, and/or emotions.

Some people see better than they feel; others, like myself, feel better than see. But there are also times I will get very clear images when praying about something or just when God brings something to my attention. Never predetermine through what vehicle and how God will speak to you. You must remain open and attentive to His leading. However, He always will give you an assurance within your heart to confirm it. When the Lord speaks, it will never be in fear, confusion, anxiety, or contradiction of His Word. His presence and leading is always in peace, love, and rest. Confusion only comes when you have self-serving motives or desires (James 3:16).

God does not speak to us with the tongues of man. He doesn't use Spanish, English, or German to talk to us. Nor does He use our physical mind as the source of His communication. It is through the channel of our heart that the Lord speaks. And it is the heart that speaks the universal language of signs, symbols, visions, dreams, feelings, and/or emotions.

We as modern man have given dominance to our intellectual mind and have regarded the feelings of the heart as childish and immature. It is time we begin to value and put precedence on the heart more than on logical reasoning. If we are to be led by the Spirit of God, then we too ought to become highly acute in awareness of the medium by which He speaks. Even if God uses nature or another person to speak to us, the Lord always does so with the attachment of the heart. It is just like when I told the story of Andrea and the grasshopper in Volume 1. The grasshopper did not open his mouth and talk; rather, the Holy Spirit used it symbolically to get her attention to what He was speaking within her heart. The same also applies when people speak into our life through the inspiration of the Holy Spirit. They may not even be aware God is using them. But, when we hear their words, the Lord uses those words to connect with what He was speaking on the inside of us through the heart. We must learn this language and become as comfortable using the language of heart as we do our physical forms of communication of everyday life. It is challenging and a little awkward at first when learning any language. However, we must become fluent in this language of the heart.

I am constantly challenging myself and growing in the language of heart and spirit. I am often asking myself in regards to thoughts, feelings, and emotions if they are the Holy Spirit speaking to me, my human spirit self speaking, just my emotions getting carried away, or the thoughts of my heart speaking. The only way to learn is to continually pray (communicate) with the Lord and to commune in your heart as to what is going on and why. Like learning any language, it takes time. Each of us has to learn the clarity and authoritative yet gentle leading of the Holy Spirit. Yet, you also need to learn how to discern the difference between His leading versus you own personal heart's desires, and so on.

Allow me to break this down a little further into everyday reality. As a youth I was desperate to become proficient when listening to the voice of the Holy Spirit. I wanted to be used by God in a powerful way, but I did not have anyone to disciple me in learning to hear His voice in ordinary everyday life. Really, I lacked the guidance to listening from the heart. It is hard to break the addiction of analyzing, defining, and logically thinking everything through the filter of the brain, which only serves to complicate the simplicity of awareness through the heart.

I told God I was willing to do anything He asked. I drove up to people's homes and knocked on their doors to relay what I thought I heard the Lord speaking. I talked to strangers and practiced like this for a time, but it resulted in great failure—or so I thought. I was beside myself feeling as if I was not worthy for God to speak to, and when I thought He did, it appeared to prove otherwise. The problem was that I did not learn how to quiet myself within. In hindsight I can see now that I was hearing the Lord, but I was distorting the message through my thoughts and personal opinions of what I thought God would probably say. I rushed the communication and came up with a hastened rationalized message. Fortunately, I did not quit. Many believers step out to practice what they believe they heard God speak to them, but after a few attempts that did not seem fruitful they tend to quit. Brothers and sisters, I encourage you to never quit. Learning the language of heart and spirit within today's culture is like learning a foreign language. With enough practice and patience, you too can become fluent in the language of heart.

QUIETING THE WATERS WITHIN

Be still, and know that I am God....

Psalm 46:10, emphasis added

Stand in awe, and sin not: commune with your own heart upon your bed, and be still.

Psalm 4:4 KJV, emphasis added

The concept of stillness is nearly unheard of in the Western world. I must take a moment and present the aspect of stillness, or silence, which I consider to be quite sacred. It is not that this silence is magical in this sense; the silence is merely the doorway.

Quieting yourself to listen with absolute purity is like a pond. Imagine that this pond is crystal clear and calm. The surface is serene and flat like glass. You can see the reflection of every tree, plant, and even the birds flying overhead along with the detail of their colors in the pond's surface imagery. Now, imagine a light breeze blowing over the surface of the water. Notice how the reflection shatters into a thousand little pieces. You still see trees and larger details, but it lacks the sharpness and even smaller things like the birds flying overhead and the plant imagery. The pond signifies your heart at its pure state. The breeze represents your thoughts.

Similar to when I thought I heard the Lord speak to me about various people in my early years of learning to hear His voice, I distorted the message He was speaking. God was speaking to me, but I had so many thoughts that I was not clear and at total peace trying to decipher what exactly I was feeling impressed about. So, in my zeal, I acted on what I thought God was speaking. I can remember getting about half correct when I received feedback from those I practiced on in this manner. You see, I did not know how to slow down, let go of myself, and wait for the message in my spirit to seep into my heart and soul for my logical mind to be able to interpret. Once an impression comes, you may not know how to define what you are even feeling. Don't rush! Just allow yourself time to let that feeling seep in until your mind can identify what your heart is feeling.

> *Allow yourself time to let that feeling seep in until your mind can identify what your heart is feeling.*

When your mind connects to what your spirit or the Holy Spirit is trying to speak, there is an elated sense of peace. It is similar to taking a road trip. Say you have packed your bags and the car is loaded, but you keep feeling like you are forgetting something. You pause for a moment and go over your checklist, but everything you planned for is packed so you shrug it off. Just before you leave, the feeling that you are forgetting something hits you again. You can't figure out what it is, so again you blow it off. Now you are driving down the road and the feeling arises, but it is much lighter this time. You don't pay much attention as you turn on the dash light and bingo! You realize that you forgot your flashlight! The dash light symbolically connected with your mind regarding the feeling you were sensing and the connection of forgetting your flashlight hit home. That nagging feeling then had a sigh of relief, but now you are left without what you forgot.

Our logical mind connects us to the physical world, whereas the spiritual mind connects us to the world of spirit. For whatever reason, religion tries to understand, communicate, and function in the realm of spirit through the logical mind. This is a carnal approach to spiritual truths. Because we are both a spirit and a physical being, we need to be able to operate out of both minds. As we grow in the Lord, we will begin to find ourselves viewing the world through the physical senses, then with a shift of consciousness view it through the spiritual senses. Eventually, we will be able to fuse the two minds together and view the world through the physical and spiritual simultaneously.

We have relied far too heavily on external pacifiers to assist us in our relationship with God. Our meditation must be simple and pure. Am I saying to abandon pacifiers for quieting the physical mind or toss the crutches that aid in inspiring us? Absolutely not! I am saying we must mature and grow up so we can become an aid to others and help lead them into intimacy with Jesus no matter the time or circumstance. This way daily life changes from stagnant to dynamic.

SILENCE OF THE SEEP

Imagine watering a fruit tree that grows in a garden. Either you pour water from a bucket or you place a garden hose nearby and let the water run for a few minutes. Either way, you would notice the water pool up around the tree and then gradually seep into the earth. Now I ask you, how did the water soak into the soil? Did the earth grow muscles and suck the water down?

Just as that is an absurd question, so too is it absurd to think we have to somehow suck an answer out of God when we communicate with Him or are simply in conversation with Him. Just like the water naturally seeps into the soil around the tree, so we are to allow His voice to seep from our spirit, through our heart, and imprint on our soul. Whenever I rush the process of hearing His voice, I nearly always distort the message. Don't get me wrong;

I often hear an immediate answer, but when I am stressed or not at peace internally, is when I generally need the extra time to meditate on His voice.

After we quiet the waters within, so to speak, we then must allow for the *process* of communication. For example, we may have some serious questions that need answering. Before we speak to the Lord about them, we will boil down the questions into their pure essence. It is similar to putting the "quest" back into the "question." The more vague or specific the question, the more vague or specific the answer. Once we quiet down and enter that "secret place" holding onto our question, we go before the Father and then, after a few moments, present the question. We do not need to use physical words to present the question; we can present it to Him in our heart while in that heart-conscious state. Then, after we let go of the question, we sit in that place of silence waiting for an answer. The answer may come in part or as a whole, but we can rest assured that the Lord will speak. That is His promise to you and me.

The faith in prayer is the releasing of that prayer. It is when you believe enough that you fully surrender the prayer to God, letting go of the need and not holding on to it anymore. Then you make yourself like a blank slate before Him, letting go of all prejudice, preconceived ideas, and personal thoughts. When the Holy Spirit speaks to you, sometimes you know there is a stirring or nuance in your heart, but you lack the words to describe what has changed. That is okay. Let go of your need to analyze and define. Allow the word to seep into your soul. As that word seeps into your soul, it will metamorphose into thought that the mind can understand. Sometimes I have asked God about things and had only a fragment of an answer in response. I never doubted He would answer in the right timing. Sometimes it would be six months to a year later that I would have a complete answer. These things are not bad. There are times you ask for answers that you are not yet ready to handle the answer to. You and I are in a growing process, and it is this process that is a hope of everyday life.

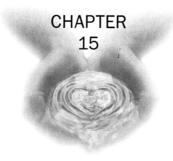

THOUGHTS OF THE HEART

*Thus says the LORD of hosts: "Do not listen to the words of the prophets who prophesy to you. They make you worthless; **they speak a vision of their own heart**, not from the mouth of the LORD. They continually say to those who despise Me, 'The LORD has said, "You shall have peace"'; and to everyone who walks according to the dictates of his own heart, they say, 'No evil shall come upon you.'"*

Jeremiah 23:16-17 emphasis added

*How long will this be in the heart of the prophets who prophesy lies? Indeed they are **prophets of the deceit of their own heart**.*

Jeremiah 23:26, emphasis added

When learning the language of heart, it is paramount that we learn to identify the thoughts of our own heart. Jesus said that evil imaginations proceed from the heart. Now, our heart is not a bad thing; but when we take a thought, begin to meditate on it, and imagine what it would feel like to experience that thought, then those imaginations take place within the heart. In order for that to happen, we would have had to allow some crooked thought pass through our established filters and make its home in our beliefs. That imagination, mixed with the emotions it creates, then begins to alter our beliefs.

For example, our culture promotes promiscuity as a means of happiness. If some people save their virginity until marriage, they are looked upon as strange in today's society. We have a culture that looks everywhere for fulfillment externally but rejects the responsibility of choice that begins internally. It is a fact that most everyone is in *pursuit* of happiness. Happiness as a goal to pursue then becomes some illusive target that can never be reached. No matter how much is attained or experienced, we have a very unsatisfied and distracted world around us. To many, life is nothing more than material gain.

I started to mention promiscuity as a means of satisfaction. When people begin to look externally for fulfillment, they are thinking about one thing: self. They are not giving back according to the abundance of life in them; they are looking to take, in hopes of finding pleasure to fill the state of lack they are in. If we take a thought by saying that we need this or that to find contentment, then we are persuading our heart that we are in lack. The more we dwell on something we need or the more we stress about things out of our reach, the more we convince our heart beliefs that we are lacking in that area.

The Bible tells us in James that all temptation comes from a sense of lack. When we are drawn away to believe we need something outside of God for fulfillment, that is when we fall into deception and temptation. The examples of prophets prophesying out of their own heart, and the times Jesus said that evil imaginations, murders, adulteries, thefts, and so on come from the heart, were all because man was in a condition of lack.

RIGHT, YET WRONG

I want to point out something that confused me for several years. I knew a couple of evangelists who worked powerfully in the Holy Spirit. They operated in words of knowledge unlike things I had ever seen. When they heard from the Lord, it was amazingly accurate every time. However, both of these men, although they were pinpoint accurate with words of knowledge and prophecy, would greatly miss in a particular area of prophecy. I was confused by seeing someone so mightily used in prophecy, yet totally miss it in one area. I couldn't understand how someone who knew God's voice so well could misinterpret His voice in these areas. It baffled me and caused me to wonder if I could ever truly know the Lord's voice without making mistakes. Until that day...

After some time had gone by, the Lord showed me these scriptures in Jeremiah. Instantly I got that *rhema* word that inspired my spirit with understanding. These men of God did indeed hear His voice in certain areas, but they were confusing His voice with the voice of their own heart when they misrepresented God in the areas in which they were not accurate. God speaks to us through the channel of our heart, so His voice often sounds much like our own. By speaking through the channel of our heart, His voice filters through our personality; thus, we often hear God speak to us much like we think to ourselves. The difference in hearing the voice of the Holy Spirit is that deep peace that accompanies His voice. Also, there is the sense of inspiration in which we know that we know, but we don't quite know how we know. Allow me to use a scripture in the book of James to help clarify:

> For where envy and self-seeking exist, confusion and every evil thing are there.
>
> James 3:16

We can be confused in hearing God's voice only when we have our selfish ambitions involved. Both the men of God I am speaking of did indeed have reasons to prophesy in error because of their personal emotional involvement in their particular misunderstanding. This is the same as the prophets Jeremiah referred to. So did this principle apply to the imaginations (or meditations) of the heart Jesus spoke of? These vain imaginations from the individual's heart were because of a personal motivation in one way or another.

Did you notice in Jeremiah 23 how the prophets were deceived? This would indicate that they thought they were hearing God, when in reality they were hearing the thoughts of their own heart. They did see a vision, but it was not inspired by God; rather, it was a vision that came from the prophet's personal heart. How? Let's read on.

INTERPRETING MOTIVATION

Jesus said that the pure in heart would see (perceive) God. There is no confusion in your heart if you have pure intentions. However, when you mix your motives with personal agendas outside of God, that is when confusion can take hold and the voice of the Holy Spirit gets distorted. Often people then make an excuse, saying that they can never know God's voice, because of failed attempts. If you are honest with yourself, the confusion you have caused is nearly always because you approach His guidance with some preconceived notion or personal want. Then it is no longer about a servant mentality, but a selfish ambition.

When we see a vision in our heart that is not from God, or if we think thoughts in our heart that are not from God, it is because of what we allowed in. For example, if I am constantly meditating on a perceived sense of lack in finances, relationships, or some other dependency on something to fulfill my happiness, I then would be establishing my heart in this belief. My heart then would do everything in its power to bring those things into my life to bring the perceived peace and wholeness. After just a little time spent doing this, my heart will declare to me that these imagined things are necessary. Since I may be familiar with the language of the heart in hearing God's voice in the areas where I do not have ulterior motives, I then must be aware of when my motives get in the way and pollute the purity of God's leading.

With a little practice one can begin to learn to identify how he or she is interpreting the thoughts of the heart. Just like Jesus asked the young lawyer, "What is written in the law?" and "How do you interpret it?", we must ask what is written in our heart and why we perceive what we do in the way we do. We must pay attention to what we perceive the Lord speaking to us, then ask ourselves if we had any personal motives in hearing the Lord the way we did!

Just a little practice and awareness of these truths will change the way we walk in our heart forever. As long as we maintain the attitude of a disciple, we can learn to deftly operate from the heart in the same manner Jesus demonstrated for us. Let's learn to pay attention to what we normally wouldn't have paid attention to.

The question is,
what is your heart motivation?

Yes, we are to ask and receive from the Lord. The question is, what is your heart motivation? Are you seeking God to bless your business for personal gain, or is it to establish and build the Good News covenant through Jesus, being a light in the midst of darkness around you? Simply put, are your motivations for self, or are they for a greater purpose beyond self to enrich others? Prosperity in material possessions can be either good or evil. Financial wealth motivated by love is to reach out and bless those around you. Financial wealth motivated by ego only breeds greed and discontentment, lusting for more, which has destroyed countless families and lives. It is selfish, however, to desire to be poor. How? If your motivation is to have just enough for you and your family, then you have no love to help and bless those around you. Are you praising God for the unmerited favor poured out on you so you can boost your ego, or do you use His favor as a testimony to encourage and bless others around you? James 4:3 says you don't receive what you desire because you desire in a manner outside of God.

For the word of God is living and powerful, and sharper than any two-edged sword, piercing even to the division of soul and spirit, and of joints and marrow, and is a discerner of the thoughts and intents of the heart.
Hebrews 4:12

The Word of God always proves the intentions and motives of your heart. Jesus was a master at bringing forth people's intentions. Consider the time He asked the lawyer, "What is written in the law? What is your reading of it?" Then a short while later the lawyer wanted to justify himself, which promoted another question. How about you? Is there something in your heart that reads the Word trying to prove your own interpretations and justifications? Or do you read the Word through proper filters, being willing to change? The filters are in accordance to the life and ministry of Jesus, the accomplished finished work of the cross, and your position in Christ today. How are you interpreting the Word? Even more importantly, why? That question alone will reveal your heart motives and intentions. Only you are able to answer that question within yourself. You may fool everyone on the outside, but those answers lie within your own heart.

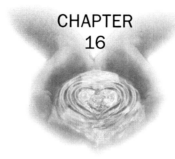

STRONGHOLDS

For the weapons of our warfare are not carnal but mighty in God for
pulling down strongholds, casting down arguments and every high thing
that exalts itself against the knowledge of God, bringing every thought
into captivity to the obedience of Christ, and being ready to punish all
disobedience when your obedience is fulfilled.

2 Corinthians 10:4-6

First, I would like to begin by saying that not all strongholds
are negative. There are many Godly strongholds that the Bible
encourages us to create as a safe harbor, or place of safety, within
our heart. David made Zion his stronghold in 2 Samuel 5:7. On numerous
occasions David referred to God as his stronghold and place of refuge. A
great example is the strength David was able to acquire when he encouraged
himself in the Lord. The people wanted to stone him, but due to the positive stronghold he had established in his heart, he was able to turn the tables.
Thus, instead of failure, there was great victory because of his decision and
stronghold in the Lord (1 Samuel 30).

Getting back to 2 Corinthians 10:4-6, we find a particular scripture that
has been greatly abused in a host of manners within the body of Christ. A

stronghold is simply something you find yourself doing repeatedly. For example, you may be working on changing your behavior by sheer will power, but
when your guard is down you find yourself repeating the very thing you did
not wish to do. Another way to describe it is like a default system. That would
be a stronghold. The strength of a stronghold is the strength of its emotions.[1]

*A stronghold is simply something you
find yourself doing repeatedly.*

I am not teaching on spiritual warfare. Nevertheless, every scripture that
deals with spiritual warfare deals with the mind. If you look at the Word
without past prejudices and study what spiritual warfare is in its purity, you
will find that the real battle is over your perceptions and beliefs. I must, however, move on to the power of strongholds.

We all make emotional decisions based on pain or pleasure. The established beliefs we hold are what we, in our perception, believe to bring us
the most pleasure with the given resources available to us. This is where our
perception can make or break us. We must have a conditioned heart to see
(perceive) life, peace, and reward in any circumstance. Let's take Jesus' example of perceiving pleasure while enduring the cross: "Looking unto Jesus the
author and finisher of our faith; *who for the joy that was set before him endured
the cross*, despising the shame, and is set down at the right hand of the throne
of God" (Hebrews 12:2 KJV, emphasis added).

When Jesus endured the cross, His focus was not on the cross itself.
Rather, Jesus was focusing on the reward of what the cross would produce
for all of eternity. He saw the joy and life that would come from that work.
He perceived the beatings and shame as no comparison to what the reward
would be. So, we could further say that His bearing the cross was possible by
His perceiving the pleasure.

We are encouraged as believers through Jesus' example to have patience
and see the overall reward of our faith and walk with God. We are to see
that although hard times may come and storms may blow around us, if we

1 For more information on spiritual warfare, I recommend you read Dr. James B. Richard's book, *Satan
Unmasked* (Huntsville, Alabama: MileStones International Publishers, 2004).

will hold on with patience, we will reap our reward that has eternal benefits. On the other hand, the quick gratifications of the flesh for today may bring short-lived pleasure, but their end is death. We must be a people of vision like Jesus and allow the processes of life to work in and around us.

We were created to live in a state of peace. Man was created in paradise and was designed to live in that environment. Since the natural paradise has been subjected to the curse of death, we as spiritual people must learn that the condition of our soul is not based on external circumstances falling in perfect order. Instead, the prosperity of our soul is to live from the Kingdom within us, which in turn will transform how we view and walk in the external life around us. Even if we did live in the Garden of Eden, the same principle would apply. Adam and Eve had a perfect external environment, yet they still managed to lose their joy and happiness. There was no lack in their lives externally. Howbeit, because they changed their internal perception, they viewed paradise as not enough.

HOW TO READ THE HEART

Think of Eve for a moment in the Garden of Eden with the talking snake. Satan deceived her with the same lie he believed got him kicked out of heaven. Satan, as an angel, was called Lucifer and was blessed with great beauty and splendor. Even though he was created with such elegance and was given an honorable position, Lucifer began to feel a sense of lack. Or you could say he began to feel a loss of fulfillment. Remember that angels are ministering spirits. They were created to be servants in various capacities, and the Bible is clear that Lucifer got caught up in his self-centeredness, in which he became blinded to a higher purpose and call. Lucifer lost touch with the joy and love of God and acted on the stirring emotions he had inside of him. Had Lucifer identified what he was feeling and approached God to share what was at work within his heart, is it possible he could have had a different outcome?

Now, take a look at what the talking snake was doing to Eve in the Garden. That snake was planting lack in Eve's heart in order to get her to respond to those new inward feelings of the heart. Often, we are unaware that we have limited information, and then with that limited information we process our beliefs to line up with a misperception that we think is accurate. Had Eve been aware of her change of perception and a shift in the subtle feelings within her own heart, she could have told the snake to meet her back at the tree that same time tomorrow to discuss further the case he was presenting— after she went and told God how she was feeling and hear what He had to say about the matter. This is exactly how we read what is going on within the heart realm. If you want to know what is in your heart, pay attention to how you are feeling. Sincerely, ask yourself, "How am I feeling?" Then if you want to know *why* you are feeling that way in order to correct it or expound on it, then take a moment and sincerely and gently ask yourself "Why?" If you want to perceive something externally from you, maybe a person, place, or thing, ask yourself, "How does this make me feel?" Pause in that place of silence and sense the impression or unction, and sometimes imagery that returns.

When we embrace a negative stronghold, it is because we believe that to be our way for the most pleasure and peace. Whenever the Bible talks about spiritual warfare, it is talking about the battlefield within our mind. If my consciousness is somewhere out on external things, then I can never know the Kingdom of God. The Kingdom of God is an internal realm and is experienced internally. We tend to rarely experience Christ in us because often we do not place our awareness of Him within us.

The Bible in 2 Corinthians 10:4-6 is not trying to stop us from thinking or to stop bad thoughts. It says to take them into captivity to the obedience of Christ. We are in control of *what* we think about and *how* we will think about it. So, we can take a thought or something that seems more esteemed than God, whether arguments, feelings, thoughts, or any other thing, and check it in light of Christ's obedience. Every thought or stronghold must be evaluated by our covenant with God through Jesus' obedience. Changing our thoughts won't win the battle; changing how we feel will.

Changing our thoughts won't win the battle;
changing how we feel will.

The problem with positive thinking is that it works only as long as we are thinking positive. It is our belief systems that we must change. Once we change our beliefs, then our feelings will change according to those beliefs. Then, once the feelings are changed, our actions will follow. No one can consistently make decisions greater than the emotions he or she feels.

When you were a child and afraid of the dark, it was not the thought of darkness that terrified you; it was the emotions and feelings that accompanied that thought about monsters that scared you. Darkness in and of itself has no power to induce fear if there is no feeling attached to it. But, the moment you meditate on "what if" or all of the worst-case scenarios, then fear has place.

Let's take a look at verse 6 again: "And being ready to punish all disobedience when your obedience is fulfilled." This is one of those verses where you really cannot rely on your King James English to help in understanding the interpretation from the Greek. As I studied it out with my concordance, I found that this scripture translates more accurately as such: "And having readiness (preparedness) to punish (vindicate your rights; reclaim) all disobedience (inattention) when (till) your obedience (attentive hearkening) is fulfilled (perfected)."

You could read it like this: "Have preparedness to vindicate what is rightfully yours that was lost through inattentiveness so that your awareness may be complete."

The strongholds are the arguments and things we believe that are in opposition to God. So we must reclaim those parts of our life where we believed something contrary to what Jesus accomplished on the cross.

ASSOCIATIONS

A stronghold is created by an association. What you feel about memories or imaginations are based on associations. Suppose a young boy growing up in South Africa constantly is warned by his mother to keep away from snakes. The mother may have a good reason to instill a healthy respect for these reptiles, especially since toddlers don't know how to differentiate between the venomous from the non-venomous. Now let's say that every time a snake shows up, his momma snatches him up and runs for cover in an irrational blind panic. As he grows into an adult, if this man acts irrationally every time a snake appears, that would be due to the association of his mother screaming and snatching him away at the sight of a distant snake. However, as an adult he must change that association to break the stronghold of the phobia, which is an irrational fear.

In another example, suppose you went to work for a good friend. However, once employed by your good friend, you find yourself beginning to distrust and have bad feelings toward him or her. That friend may have done nothing wrong, but somehow you are feeling distant and you don't have the same affection for the person as you did prior to working for him or her. As you look in your heart, you may find that as a child you had an abusive parent and you are now associating your friend as an authority figure like your parent was. This again is a stronghold that must be dealt with in order for your life to come into wholeness. Everyone is different, but no matter what works the best for you, you must put off the old and put on the new.

Finally, say a woman as a young girl saw her father abandon her and her mother. She may create a stronghold through an inner vow saying that she will never allow herself to be hurt by a man again. In that passionate moment she says men are not to be trusted, for they will find any reason to be unsatisfied and leave the family. Let's then say she forgot about the stronghold she created through faulty beliefs as a child and gets married. She had a great dating relationship with her new husband, but after her honeymoon night everything changed. This woman, for some irrational reason, grows callous and hard toward her new husband. The association was that her boyfriend was now in a lifelong committed relationship, one in which she believed no man was capable of keeping. The husband became an association to trigger the deep-rooted beliefs of the past that were never dealt with.

If you know of some area in your life where you act irrationally, ask yourself this question: "Why?" What was the first time you felt that sense of whatever you are feeling? From there bring those feelings and associations into alignment with Jesus' obedience regarding the matter. Feel what Jesus feels about those things and allow Him to change your perception and experience about the matter. Ask Jesus what He thinks about the situation. Further, ask Him how you should view the issue; then ask for a plan to walk into healing from the situation.

We must be on guard as to what is influencing our emotions and feelings. There are many sources of information bombarding us every day in all manner of ways. Even television can become a source for creating associations if we are not careful. Television is actually considered to be a modern day opiate. When we sit in front of the TV, it is like using an opiate that engages our mind into a low alpha state. The low alpha is not the productive high alpha we desire. Rather, it lulls us like a drug. It is our responsibility to pay attention to the effect TV or any influence is having on us.

We must be on guard as to what is influencing our emotions and feelings.

Let's say you are engaged in some show where atrocities are taking place and the character you find yourself connecting to is wronged. Then that character commits some act to get revenge and is later justified and even rewarded in some one-night romantic getaway. You can feel how good it is to have revenge on those who wronged you and the pleasure of that one-night stand of romance that will be forever a cherished memory. In connecting with fornication and malice in a pleasurable manner, you are to some degree creating emotions that tell your heart there is a time and place to disregard what God says, that it is okay to follow your own path for fulfillment. The focus of what you should be on guard for is not whether or not this is right or wrong, but rather "How is this affecting my heart?"

Return to the stronghold, you prisoners of hope. Even today I declare that I will restore double to you.

Zechariah 9:12

As I said earlier, not all strongholds are negative. David talked greatly about the Lord as his *stronghold*, refuge, and safety in 2 Samuel 22:2-3. The secret place of the heart where the Almighty dwells is to be our safe harbor. It is our place of safety, security, and rest. Chapter 11, "Guarding and Establishing the Heart," talks about establishing our heart in grace, righteousness, and hope, which is, in reality, creating a stronghold of grace, righteousness, and hope.

We need to connect with Christ *in us* in order to have the hope of glory at work in our members. An example of prosperity would be when we meditate on, thus experiencing, prosperity working in your life, we create an association with the feelings and awareness of that state of being. With a little time it becomes a positive stronghold in our heart. As we continue to meditate and connect to the truth of God's Word at work in our life, we develop a subconscious strength in that area.

ENVISIONING

I had mentioned that the more powerfully we experience an emotion mixed with a perceived belief of why, we create or strengthen a stronghold— whether good or bad. Prayer and fasting together has prevailing lasting effects because of this very principle. When we pray (commune with God) and fast (deny our physical desires), we are persuading our heart to God's reality in the spirit. Our body and mind experience hardship, but we affirm our belief that the physical world is not our focus regardless of how we feel. The heightened emotional experience of discomfort burns into our soul. We then take that discomfort to strengthen our belief that the flesh is weak and not to be trusted. The spirit is our source for strength and insight. It is a way we keep the physical body submitted to the will and mind of the spirit. We, in fact, are creating a positive stronghold on the rock of Jesus and the reality of His Kingdom at work within the world around and in us.

Envisioning is a powerful aspect of prayer. The Bible declares that God sees and knows all the imaginations of our heart. He is aware of our deepest core. Our thoughts and imaginations are always before Him. One way to pray is to consciously think or ponder in the presence of the Lord. What we are saying is, "Father, I am purposefully meditating or thinking in front of You. I ask and know that You will help me in my thinking process of this thing I am pondering. I am fully yielded to Your interjections and give You authority over all that I meditate on." Communing with God also is thinking within our heart about a matter or just putting our awareness on His presence while being open to anything He speaks to us.

Envisioning is a powerful aspect of prayer.

Because God uses the language of heart to speak to us, we too must use this language to communicate back. Words are a manifestation of what we are feeling or seeing within our heart. Romans 10 says that it is the heart that has the ability to believe. The heart is what perceives and believes. Then it is the words of the mouth that manifest the completion of that salvation. The words of the mouth plainly speak out of the abundance of what is in the heart. So the true power is that which is working within us (Ephesians 3:20).

Envisioning is vastly different from visualization. Visualization is like looking at a photograph or quick movie clip, but it lacks the personal emotional experience. Envisioning is when what you are imagining becomes so real that you find yourself living that experience, albeit through envisioning. It works to the positive or negative. On the positive side, maybe you are praying for someone. As you envision that person healed, saved, delivered, or whatever else, you can feel the excitement and joy that he or she is experiencing. That then becomes a powerful form of intercession.

One word of caution: Do not envision in a way that limits God to moving in only one perceived expectation. The Bible says to expect God to hear and answer your prayer when you pray and to use your authority in accordance to His will. Howbeit, you are not to limit the way and manner in which He will move. The bottom line is that God will continue to be faithful and that you and I are right to expect good from Him. It is just that you don't always have the capacity to know the overall picture and through what means He may answer you. Each situation is different. You cannot know what is in other people's hearts. Only God knows the hearts of men and women. Only He knows how and where to lead His people into the abundant life. Your job is to just keep your eyes and focus on Jesus.

So, what does envisioning have to do with associations? Envisioning can create or destroy a stronghold. Envisioning can become so real that it is hard to distinguish between that which was envisioned and that which is physical reality. A stronghold is formed through a perceived experience or reality. So, by using the envisioning process to our aid, we can change the course of our life. We can create a reality based on the promises and truth of God's Word, where we actually experience the end from the beginning. For example, if I am sick and lying in bed, I would envision myself up and walking. I would see and experience the completion of my healing. I would sense the feeling of peace and wholeness in my body. I would experience that end before I physically saw any manifestation. By doing so, I would be persuading my heart that healing is already mine and that I don't have to go chase after it. I would be positioning my heart to yield to the grace of Jesus to move from the spiritual reality through my heart, through my soul, and into my body. If we are to experience any prosperity and health physically, we must first learn to experience it in the soul (3 John 2; 1 Peter 1:9).

APPLICATION

Allow me to share a couple of recent examples of envisioning that I have used to break addiction and in the area of healing in my back. Most everyone has either seriously dealt with deals with some form of addiction, a driven craving that is in some way or how controlling. Some of the most familiar forms of addiction we tend to think of are those like chewing tobacco, cigarettes, alcohol, sex, and drugs. Addictions come in all sorts and sizes. One of my friends only allows himself a certain brand of pizza four times a year because of the addictive craving he fights to overeat when it is in his presence. I personally have had to deal with an addiction to a certain soda. I don't want to fight an addiction all of my life, struggling with wanting something that I know is killing me or holding some kind of power over me. So that is when I go to the heart. To me, drinking a daily dose of my favorite soda is like drinking sweet yummy death. Even though I knew it was bad for me, my body craved it like it would crave any other form of nutrition it needed; I was addicted to the caffeine and sugar. Thus, I chose to rewrite the pleasure I associated with this soda with the reality of pain it was causing beneath the surface. The way I did this was to find a condition of what I associated to a healthy, strong, and pure body. It may sound funny to you, but the image of a lean and healthy body I have is the image of a North American Indian from the 1600s or 1700s drinking from cupped hands out of a fresh water spring. That purity and freshness of water entering the native's body to rejuvenate his strength is what I think of. So, I took this image from my mind and then compared it with drinking soda. The syrupy liquid that creates an environment for every sort of disease, I looked at it like it was a bottle of antifreeze. Off and on as my thirst came I would think about how pure and refreshing water was, which then would trigger how much I thought that soda was like antifreeze. I envisioned myself hot and thirsty, then taking a long drink of crystal clear water, which would restore my strength and clarity of mind without the caustic chemicals working their harm in my gut and energy level. After meditating off and on in this manner for a little over a week, I was free from the strong desire to drink this soda. With a little sincere effort the addiction broke, and now I am not fighting a difficult and often defeated battle doing what I don't want to do, and now doing what I want to do. What we write in our heart will become the compass that directs our life.

This heart principle works in every area of life, including physical healing. Not long ago I was overworking my body building a barn and tore both lower back muscles in my back. It hurt so bad I couldn't walk, stand, or do anything! The pain was so intense I was sweating and short of breath just from the injury alone. The first tendency is just to lie down and try to sleep it off. A physical ailment like this tends to take the life and energy out of us, leaving us paralyzed physically and mentally. It is in these times we cannot allow our authority to be taken from us and yield to passivity. Driving to the job the next morning with very minute improvement, I had one-half hour to get my healing manifested. I was in a situation where I really was not facing a good alternative if I did not get to work and finish my responsibilities. While driving early the next morning, I reevaluated my right to healing through Jesus' stripes. I then reviewed in my heart how I am one with Jesus and He with me. My body is His body, which means my muscles are His muscles and His muscles are my muscles. Long story short, I took about 20 minutes persuading and affirming my own heart that I had every right and justification to believe for healing of torn muscles in such a short amount of time. From this standpoint I then very firmly and authoritatively envisioned. I first felt the pain, then I imagined a shape to what the pain I was feeling looked like. I then imagined that shape as pitch black. All of the pain and discomfort was associated in that which I was imagining in my back. I then shrunk that black shape down into a tiny little pea-sized ball. All the intense pain was now capsulated within that tiny ball. I then imagined Jesus on the cross, as if reliving an old memory. Then, I sent that tiny ball out of my back and onto the body of Jesus. The pain alleviated a bit, and I repeated the process a couple more times until I was no longer aware of the pain. I worked all of that day without even thinking about my back! I was so focused on the project at hand that I did not realize how free I was until that night at home reflecting on the day. By doing this little exercise I was taking authority and commanding my body to be healed. By shrinking the original shape of the problem to a tiny little sphere, I was making it into what it really is in light of Jesus' finished work. This may seem a little unorthodox, but that is what works well for me when I need to take command over my body. I often work in a gift of healing when praying for others, but when I need healing in my own body, I must work in my own authority as a believer.

You will always know once you step over from simple visualizing to the power of envisioning from the place of faith. We can quote the Bible all day long, but until it is mixed with faith it produces no results (Hebrews 4:2). The earmark of knowing if you are in that "place" of faith or not is through the inner awareness of the heart. As you pray or meditate on God's Word, you may begin to experience the end from the beginning. Once that happens, you are there. What I am referring to is experiencing the joy and gratitude as if you already have in physical possession that which you seek or intercede for. You cannot pretend thankfulness. It is genuine or it is nothing at all. In our human logic we think we are not supposed to express joy and thankfulness until after we receive the fullness of that which we seek or believe. Nothing could be further from the truth. In the spiritual laws of faith, we know according to Hebrews 11 that faith is the substance of things hoped for. A more accurate translation of that is to say, "…faith is the title of ownership of things…." So, once we touch that place of faith, we can know we have ownership. Once we have ownership, we will find that time means nothing. Whether today, tomorrow, or next year until we see full manifestation, it does not matter because we know it is ours. That is where patience becomes so easy; it is really a non-issue. Altogether herein is the earmark. As you meditate and pray, once you genuinely begin to feel gratitude and joy stir within the core of your heart, you have touched faith. Faith then is mixing with the Word. Under no circumstances allow anyone or anything to steal your joy. Do not run and look at the external circumstances to see if there is a change to justify your emotions that are working in your heart. Keep your focus internal and lay hold of the promise through the heart. Allow your soul to hold on to and experience that from the heart, and watch the course of your life begin to shift and line up with that which you hold and experience within. Do not be discouraged if it takes a month or a few months before you notice external change. Time is irrelevant; results are what we are after, and true freedom—whether in seconds or days—is always worth it.

Some people may not be able to envision in a way that they see crystal-clear imagery. That is okay. If you have a hard time seeing, just focus on the feeling. That too is envisioning. If, for example, you are currently experiencing a crisis situation financially, begin to feel, or see, what it is like to experience abundance. Envision what it is like to naturally walk in prosperity. Feel what it is like to experience God's favor in your work. You can feel and experience the vision that creates to build wealth in every area of your life. Begin to feel the depressed sense of lack dissipate from your soul. Feel and maintain the freedom of the security you have in the Good Shepherd. Eventually, as you meditate on sensing the feeling of freedom in various areas of life, you will begin to envision the imagery with much greater clarity. From this place you envision in your prayer—you talk to the Lord and thank Him for opening your eyes to the opportunity and life that is all around you. The more you envision the promises of life and peace in your life, the greater the positive stronghold will become. You will find yourself abiding in the state of prosperity. Your mind will be trained to see life and opportunity. You will have created a stronghold that will become your default system, and the reason to believe is because of promises in the Word of God. No matter what disaster may try to ruin your life, you always will rise above the circumstance. Your heart will become established in the truth that life is always a choice. I must reiterate that the life I see may not be according to my personal expectations.

I must have the purity to perceive the positive apart from personal wants. I always have an expectancy of good, but what that good looks like will always be in line with God's Word.

If we cannot find the choice of life in any environment or situation, then we must change our heart beliefs. The only reason we would not be able to decide to see and live life is because we do not believe life is available. If we believe that we have to go outside of God to find the choice of life and hope, then our heart is crooked in those areas (Proverbs 17:20). So, if we find ourselves unable to perceive life and opportunity, then we have a crooked heart! This challenges me as much as anyone. God promised us the choice of life or death. Death and chaos may seem overwhelming at times, but nonetheless the choice to find good and life is always available. Often, it is easier to focus on the negative problems of life. So, if we find ourselves focusing on the chaos around us, then we need to check our heart and line our beliefs up with God's view and opinion in order to perceive the life and blessings available.

FINAL THOUGHTS

Choose to come alive from the inside out instead of the world's yo-yo philosophy of outside in. If you wake up in the morning in a bad mood, ask yourself, why? Relax and wait for the response to come. Search your soul and listen without prejudice. However, don't bother to ask the "why" if you are not going to do anything about it. You may be impressed with the thought that your co-workers are talking negatively about you at work. You may have a feeling of unsettledness toward another individual or situation. Ask the "why?" question and find out what is going on. Sometimes you may not understand what to do about it other than to pray and trust the Lord for walking the matter out. Sometimes God may give you specific and clear direction on what to do. Either way, you are on guard as to what is affecting your core, thus taking back control of your life.

There are other ways to consciously have inner awareness. From time to time, just check in and ask yourself, "How does this make me feel?" When you ask how something or someone makes you feel, then you are perceiving things in the world around you. However, if you check in and ask, "How am

I feeling?" then you are perceiving the condition of your own heart and how you personally are doing.

After expanding and contracting your awareness in such a manner, you ask the "why?" You may not always get a clear answer on the "why," but you may get a sense that you find hard to define with words. That is okay. That is when you check to follow the peace of the Lord working inside you. Always follow the peace that is working in your heart (Colossians 3:15). You may not be able to logically understand why the peace of God is inspiring you to move in a certain direction, but regardless, always obey His guidance through His peace. Satan cannot counterfeit the peace that Jesus has given you. If the voice of the enemy speaks, and if you are honest within yourself and perceive with purity, you always will sense an uneasy or unsettled feeling accompanying his thoughts or influence.

*Always follow the peace that is
working in your heart.*

For example, I heard a staggering statistic from an interview of women who had been raped. Almost one hundred percent of the women said they had a bad feeling about the date or person they were hanging out with. Others said they did not feel right about where they were going geographically, but shrugged off the "gut feeling" as an impulse. I too am learning to constantly listen to and follow the peace inside my heart. If I lose peace about a situation, I will cancel, change plans, or stop and pray about it until I feel a release to continue forward. Unfortunately, I have had to learn the hard way in many instances. I heard Andrew Wommack tell a story about a scheduled trip to Mexico. A couple weeks before the trip he began to have a strong negative feeling. The more he prayed about it, the more he lost his peace. He ended up canceling the conference in spite of the angry pastors. It was a few weeks later that Andrew saw on the news that the very plane he was scheduled to fly on had crashed, leaving no survivors. I can talk about these types of stories for hours. The point is, we need to learn how to identify and follow the peace the Lord uses to guide us, even when we in our logic want to do otherwise.

Another great way to examine your heart is to take some alone time and ask yourself, "How am I feeling?" Write down your answers on a piece of paper. At first you may get a response like "happy." Write that down, but then ask the question again. Often, your logical mind will throw in a superficial answer to keep you from dealing with your heart. For instance, you may on your second time of asking, "How am I feeling?" get a sense of anxiety. Write down "anxious." Then repeat the process again until you feel at peace that you hit the core of your feelings.

You may have anywhere from three to twenty-six answers written on a piece of paper. Just write down as many or as few as necessary until you feel a release inside that you have enough. Step two is to look through your list and pick out the two or three that stand out the most to you and circle them.

Step three is to ask yourself, "Why?" When you do this, you must surrender all thought and emotion and be like a blank slate. Don't rush this part. After asking "Why?" about one of the core feelings going on inside of you, just simply relax and let the answer seep in. It may come as an image (vision) or an impression. You even may feel your answer stirring deep within you, yet not have clarity. Don't hurry the answer. Just allow it to bubble up and connect with your mind. The answer will metamorphose from the impression in your heart into the thought of the mind.

You will find that this exercise can be a powerful and effective way to get to the root of feelings or emotions you are having. Often, you can save yourself months of internal stress or emotional confusion by doing this and dealing with your heart from the beginning. Then, once those feelings are identified, you can appropriate them in light of Jesus' obedience. Eventually, you will get proficient enough to where you can commune with your heart quite readily. You can check to see what is going on and why, deal with it according to the occasion, and change the outcome. Truly, you can consciously determine the course of your life through mastering the power of the heart.

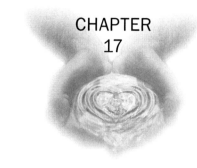

CHAPTER 17

CONCLUSION

I trust that this book has been a great source of encouragement to you and will be a future resource to understanding the heart. At the end of the day, you need to keep life simple. This work was not meant to complicate your life by any means. The hope was to take you on a journey into the realm of the heart. It is my hope to help open your eyes to look beyond the veneer of flesh. As you begin to grow and change into the complete image of who you are in Jesus, so too will your perspective on life. It is this perspective I hope to have inspired.

Living from the heart is meant to be so incredibly simple and easy that it becomes second nature. It is always a choice to read what has been written on the heart. Furthermore, the internal sense of the heart should be no different than any of the natural senses of the body. Throughout your day you use the physical senses, and you are almost oblivious to remembering what those senses experienced. One often has to stop and think about what his or her natural senses are picking up. The same is with the heart. Just like any other part of your being, you need to constantly shift your awareness. It is like consciously expanding your awareness externally and then contracting it internally throughout the day, paying attention to the things you normally don't pay attention to. Sure, the more you pay attention, the more heightened your sensitivity will become, but just like knowing a second language, if you don't use it you will forget it.

If you were talking one on one with Jesus in the flesh, how would you feel? Would your friendship be just an acquaintance or would it grow into one of deep love and affection? What would you talk about? If He just wanted a friend and companion to walk with, how would you respond?

Your response would be exactly like mine and everyone else's who believes. You would live in the moment of every day. You never would run out of things to discuss or talk about. Physical life always would include the life-giving element of spirit. You would see beyond the façade of flesh in every circumstance and environment. Life would become an everyday adventure. You would look forward to each new day and morning. Boredom would be an unknown concept. This, then, is the reality of your life when lived out of the heart. It is when you live from and never leave the Kingdom of God within you; it is when the reality of Jesus, our friend and companion, becomes the ultimate reality.

CONTACT INFORMATION

Visit our website at: www.chmin.net
Our other mailing & contact information is as follows:

Clint Herrema
P.O. Box 854
Jenison, MI 49464
(616) 805-0736

Clint Herrema is an international speaker and businessman. He and his wife Andrea reside in west Michigan. Together they minister through Clint Herrema Ministries, a successful para-church organization, through which they work alongside of the church body locally and internationally. Their ministry focus is on the areas of teaching and healing evangelism.

Passion Statement

Clint's passion is to preach, teach and demonstrate the grace of Jesus Christ, which is the power of the gospel. His mission is to pass on the message of this good news, that the world may see God glorified in every believer.

ALSO AVAILABLE BY CLINT HERREMA

Volume 1
How to Release the Power of Faith: A Field Guide to the Power of Faith

COMING SOON...

Volume 3
Walking With God: A Field Guide to Discipleship

LaVergne, TN USA
27 August 2010
194912LV00004B/2/P